M. H. Collins

Write History _Right_

A Step-by-Step Guide

Write History *Right*

How to Research, Organize and Document the Past for *your*

• **Hometown** • **Region** • **Family** • **Sports Team**
• **School** • **Events** • **Organization** • **Church**

M. H. Collins

Write History Right by M. H. Collins

Copyright © 2009

ISBN 978-0-9818346-4-1

CHS Publishing
P. O. Box 1958
Rogers, AR 72757
Orders: hswc1@cox.net

This book is intended as a guide for writers of history. The book is not intended as legal, financial, or personal advice. Advice should be acquired from an accountant or attorney. Due diligence was taken for accuracy; however, neither the author nor the publisher assume responsibility for inaccuracies or misleading information.

Quotes not attributed to other writers are by M. H. Collins

Library of Congress Control Number: 2008906691
Includes an Index

Cover design:
Lin Wellford
ArtStone Press
linwell@cswnet.com

CHS

For more information, please contact the publisher:
CHS Publishing, P. O. Box 1958, Rogers, AR 72757
479-903-6812—hswc1@cox.net
www.mhcollins.com

Dedicated to

Richard E. Markey
An Exceptional Friend

ACKNOWLEDGMENTS

I would particularly like to thank the following people for contributing their expertise to the research, writing, and publication of this book—my writing group members: Lela Davidson, Denton Gay, Lorraine Heartfield, Maeve Maddox, Mary Ann Powers, Jeannie Stone, Joe Tangari, and Barbara Youree. Barbara Youree also provided an overall editorial critique. Her positive support to my work helped keep me on task. Shirley and Dean Park were very helpful in acquiring pictures for the book. Larry Collins, my husband, never ceases to amaze me with his insight, patience, and skill.

My special appreciation also goes to Lin Wellford, ArtStone Press, for the cover design and text layout as well as her excellent overall critique and professional advice on the publication process.

Marty Jenkins, LithoPrinters, Cassville, MO, took a personal interest in the book and was very helpful in producing the final product. I greatly appreciate Tonya Wogoman for her excellent layout and Heidi Lowe for her help with the photographs.

I also thank museum directors Dr. Gaye Bland and Allyn Lord for their dedication to the preservation of history. The excellence of their work is an inspiration to me and others who share a love of history.

Photographs:
Courtesy of the Rogers Historical Museum: Pages 1,57, 62,70,73
Courtesy of Jerry Hiett: Page 35
Courtesy of Diane Hardy: Page 6
All other photos: Courtesy of the Harris/Sager family

Table of Contents

Introduction

This guide is for you if this is your first attempt at writing a book or, as a seasoned author, you are entering this genre—non-fiction history—for the first time. *Write History Right* will help make your work more professional—and easier to manage. Each chapter offers practical tips to steer you around pitfalls that can cost additional time and money.

Write History Right will guide you through all stages of writing your story—whichever topic you choose including a history of one of the following:

- Hometown
- Region
- Family
- Church
- Organizations (civic, corporate, or non-profit)
- School
- Sports team
- Military unit
- Unusual event
- Infamous and famous people

Each chapter of this book will lead you one step closer to creating, producing, and marketing your book. Chapter 1 and Chapter 2 deal with specific subjects for a history book. Chapter 1 helps you get started on a local or regional history. Chapter 2 details writing for special groups, many mentioned above.

You may find yourself working with a committee depending upon the circumstance of your book. If so, the last section in Chapter 2 will help you establish a positive working relationship with committee members.

Chapter 3 through Chapter 10 help you plan your book, set up a comfortable work schedule, develop good research sources, write professionally, decide on the best publishing method for you, and find doable ways to successfully market your book. Sample forms in the Appendix will be useful as you track and document your work.

Write History Right offers easy-to-follow suggestions that have worked well for others and for me. Using this guide will help you:

- Control overwhelming research
- Keep documentation orderly
- Make interviews more satisfactory
- Enhance the overall organization of your project into a manageable and successful undertaking

The follow-up marketing strategies are practical and doable by you, the author, whether you are launching a local or regional campaign—or selling your book to the membership of your church or organization.

I wrote this guide to help writers like you simplify the process and preserve moments in history that might otherwise never be recorded. Once a story is gone, people forgotten, and pictures or mementos stored in the attic no longer identifiable—a part of history and the role it played in our lives is lost forever.

I wish you success and hope you enjoy the pursuit of the story that stirs your passion, knowing that your contribution will be preserved for generations to come.

CHAPTER 1

Write the Story of Your Town, State, or Region

How many times have you said to someone, "I've always wanted to write a book about . . . !" *Write History Right* will change your sentiment to, "I started my book today on . . . !"

So, where do you start? We all learned historical facts and famous names in the classroom. History is textbook precise. But also messy. The "messy" parts reveal emotion, honor, deceit, or bravery that underlay the facts and may be harder to discover—but more intriguing. The richness of these details will set your story apart and add to the legacy you'll leave behind with your words.

A town—any town—is full of stories about amazing people, their world, and the incredible way they dealt with the issues of their day. Whether it was in 1807 or 2009. Look to familiar surroundings for your story.

If you don't write the story, who will?

No one else may know your chosen story better than you. If you've grown up in an area where your story takes place, you have an added advantage. However, a new arrival can sometimes see the unusual within the day-to-day stories a local person might overlook. The goal, from whichever prospective, is to take a fresh look, giving clearer meaning to stories from the past.

Find and record the lives and events that bring out the storyteller in you. You may find special insight from diaries, journals, pictures, or family stories.

Perhaps your topic has never been thoroughly researched and written in book form. For instance, if writing about a town—when and why did it begin at a certain bend of the river or become a stop for the early pony express or railroad? Who were the people with foresight to become the first settlers, start their businesses, or build their homes there? What hardships did they face? How did they overcome failure? What factors led to the town's survival or decline as seen today? Whatever the subject, add your passion.

Pictures take readers beyond the words where they can see the architecture of old buildings lined by brick streets, farmers bringing in hay, or a child throwing corn to a pen of chickens. Pictures of the everyday lives of people reveal much about the reality of the time and the way people lived, worked, and played. Gather photographs as part of your overall research.

Every place has a history

Every person, every place has a history. Your story might be found in the broad context of a wide geographic region, political movement, or a family history covering generations.

Within what boundaries will you choose to begin?

Since you will be living with your subject for several months or even longer as you write the book, choose a topic that fascinates you. The people and the circumstances of their lives should hold your interest throughout the project.

Your story might begin with the first recorded people on the land based in part on petrography left on cave walls—or artifacts preserved in dry bluffs high above rivers or along ancient transportation routes. Or with early explorers. Later settlers in this country, for whatever reason, chose a spot and put down their worldly goods saying, "This is home." You'll find their factual stories as well as evidence of their courage/cowardliness, strengths/weakness—the very essence of human history.

You don't have to always look to the distant past for a story. Yesterday's happenings are not only news, but history.

Choose the time frame, place, person, or event your book will cover. What draws you to this story? What is the story's significance to the community? Or your family?

As you look for a place to start or area to emphasize, consider the following as individual topics that might affect your story or that can be incorporated to tell a broader story. This list of suggestions is not meant to be comprehensive, but should help jump start your thinking.

Topic Ideas

- Economic influences. The Great Depression, Spanish Flu epidemic, loss of farm land due to development, impact of a new interstate highway or dam, departure of a major industry, expansion of an airport, changes in environmental law
- Natural phenomenon. Earthquake, flood, hurricane, volcano, wild fires, tornado, or drought

- <u>Effects of war</u>. Stories of individual service men/women
- <u>Famous or infamous people</u>. Writers, actors, artists, heroes/heroines, educators, religious leaders, criminals, politicians, community leaders, family members, military men and women
- <u>Cultural</u>. One-room schools, consolidation or integration of schools, influx of different customs or religions, effects of technology, fluctuation in political power
- <u>Transportation</u>. Stagecoach, riverboats, trains, cars, airplanes
- <u>The arts</u>. Early Chautauqua programs, music, art, literature, dance
- <u>Sports</u>. Horseracing, boating, baseball, football or famous sports figures.

Identify your readership

You will present your book differently depending on your primary audience. Some writers like to picture a reader that represents their target audience to keep in mind as they write. Which prospective segment (or segments) of readers do you feel your book will interest? Consider age, gender, interest level, geographic area, general or academic audience, or organization/family members.

Your largest audience will probably consist of:

- Long-time residents of the area
- New arrivals interested in the history of their new home
- Growing heritage and destination tourism market
- Area schools/libraries/bookstores

Write with your readership in mind. Include easy-to-read copy, visuals to help tell the story, unusual tales and anecdotes, and keep the writing lively and engaging.

Find and evaluate other books on your same subject that might compete for your readership. Some of this information can be found on the internet. I would also suggest talking to the local historical association director or research librarian to help identify these sources, if they exist. These resource people might also comment on the credibility and accuracy of the publication(s), or if there are areas omitted that should be addressed in your book.

> Write a short summary (25 words or so) about what you already know about the subject, why it interests you, and what kinds of questions you hope to answer through research. This brief blurb will keep the work in clear focus for you. The summary will also help to concisely explain your work to a research librarian, to people you interview, or to others you approach for information.

Analyze books you find similar to your subject. Note the following:

- Publisher—main-stream publisher, university press, local historical society or self-published
- Copyright date(s)
- Coverage of your topic
- Maps, documents, or photographs/drawings used
- Sources cited

How does your book differ from these existing publications? What sets you apart as the person to tell the most revealing and accurate story? Maybe you have original materials—journals, letters, or a diary—not available to the general public. Is there a family history or a life experience that connects you to the subject? You will use these answers to refine your thoughts as you write, seek a publisher, and later market the book.

Create a working title

Title counts. Try a play on words, strong action verbs, or use humor if appropriate to make your title more interesting. A provocative or catchy phrase will attract readers (and buyers) to your book. The title, of course, needs to honestly reflect what's inside, but use a little creativity here.

Tailor your title to the subject matter and your audience. The title and cover are your first tools in the competitive world of selling your book. The title needs to grab the reader's interest and the cover needs to appeal to the senses.

Of course, books with high author recognition will sell and sell. Without these assets, the clever writer or publisher uses words and visuals to create a buy-me cover. You may want to begin with a working title and let the final more creative one surface as you write—perhaps a phrase from the text.

Subtitles are often used to further explain the content while allowing a more interesting way to express the major title. For example, a book entitled *Two Longs and a Short* [early telephone signals] catches a reader's eye. What does this title mean? The subtitle further explains the context—*An Ozark Boyhood Remembered* (by Phillip W. Steele, Pelican Publishing Company, Inc., 2004).

The publisher may make the final title selection, but you first need to catch a publisher's interest with a strong working title.

This same advice applies to your chapter titles. Short, snappy chapter titles and subheads help draw the reader through your book. Use consistent word length and construction in your titles if possible.

This book will primarily focus on writing local and regional history, but the general principles will apply—or can be adapted—to the various other histories discussed in the next chapter.

CHAPTER 2
Write About Special Groups

The approach to research, organize, interview, write, and later market your work is much the same for special groups as for regional or local histories. However, some differences should be considered as you write in this arena. Many of these suggestions also apply to writing local and regional history.

Chapter 2 considers the unique aspects of writing a narrative or pictorial history for your church/religious group, organization, or family. Tips would also apply to a sports team, military unit, school or graduating class, or civic organization—and the list goes on.

You may find yourself working with a committee or several family members on your story—invited or perhaps indirectly invited. If so, suggestions are given at the end of the chapter to help make this process positive and to avoid possible pitfalls.

Marketing to these special groups follows much the same pattern as marketing for a regional audience. An early announcement of the project and call for input from the membership or family members help build a future base for good publicity. You might offer pre-publication sales—perhaps at a small discount—to help defray printing costs in advance of regular sales.

First of all, decide the best way to tell your story based on available material and reliable sources. Consider the following methods for organizing your book:

- Chronological. Tell the story in the order it happened.
- Topic by topic. Devote individual chapters to specific subjects (for instance, Historic Buildings, Early Leaders, Impact of Population Shifts).
- Pictorial. Tell your the thorough pictures with short descriptions (see Chapter 7).

The following suggestions will help you make the most of your opportunity for preserving the rich history of your chosen group in more detail than may be possible with an overall history of a town.

Church or religious group

Most tips are based on a typical church organization, but may also apply to the history of a synagogue, mosque, or other place of worship. Adapt the suggestions to your specific religious group.

Complete records of older churches may not have been kept in a neat, chronological order in an office. You may find conflicting dates, birth orders, and spelling of names. Marriage, birth, baptismal, and death records may have only been recorded in family Bibles or found in letters and diaries, or carved on headstones in the church or local cemetery. Photographs or other visuals throughout your book will help carry the story of people and places you highlight.

The structure of your book will probably include much of the following:

Areas To Include

- Denomination/national/international affiliation
- Name of church – any changes in name or location during the years
- Land/building/steeple/bell tower
- Cornerstone/documents
- Stained glass/art/baptismal font or baptistery/pews/ church symbols/altar/
- Communion table and vessels/vestments/choir robes and any other items of worship or art in the church
- Cemetery – include names/dates/special messages/ artwork/gate/plantings
- Financial statistics/major capital campaigns/major donors
- Church founders and charter members
- Governance (bylaws, charter, non-profit status and so forth)
- Former and current pastors/priests/rabbi/other leaders—special projects, and membership growth under their leadership
- Dedication of buildings
- Membership
- Music – choir directors/choir members/choir loft/ robes/special programs
- Musical instruments – pipe organ/piano/other
- Children/youth/adult programs
- Outreach/mission churches/mission work
- Annual events/revivals/dinner on the grounds and so forth
- Special observances relevant to your religion
- Copies of special sermons/programs
- Pictures of buildings, leaders, special events, membership
- Other details unique to your church or religion

Collect copies of former church bulletins, special celebrations/ dedications, programs, newspaper coverage, and other items of visual interest. Use the Image Records form from the Appendix and sample Release Forms to help keep track of a large number of photographs.

For organizational histories

The organization you select may be a civic, non-profit, or activist group. In any case—as with a church—the membership is your primary audience. They will have a more personal interest in the book than a general-interest readership may have.

Announce your project to the membership in advance of writing so everyone will have an opportunity to have his/her ideas considered for inclusion. Make a formal request to members for input—facts/dates, photographs, newspaper clippings, personal letters, or other information to consider for the book. You need their input before you begin writing. Set a deadline for submitting this material to you. Otherwise information may continue to trickle in creating an ongoing need to rewrite your story.

Note the tips for writing church history as many will also apply to any organization you are researching. Listed are additional items you might consider:

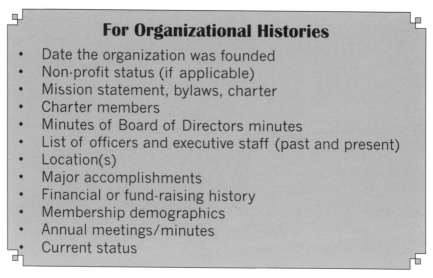

For Organizational Histories

- Date the organization was founded
- Non-profit status (if applicable)
- Mission statement, bylaws, charter
- Charter members
- Minutes of Board of Directors minutes
- List of officers and executive staff (past and present)
- Location(s)
- Major accomplishments
- Financial or fund-raising history
- Membership demographics
- Annual meetings/minutes
- Current status

Family narrative

If you are writing about a family other than your own, you will need to enlist those members for a large portion of your research. Hopefully, material will be more readily found about your own family depending on how information was collected and preserved through the years. Either way, interest in the project tends to be very personal. People want to be included. Yours is a job that is usually much appreciated. Family members want the story told but may not be in a position to produce the work themselves.

Writing a family narrative can be a little trickier than working for an organization. You might encounter objections from family members regarding using specific birth dates, inclusion of former spouses, or how you plan to handle stepchildren/step-grandchildren or adopted children. You might be requested to exclude out-of-favor family members.

How you handle such controversies is, of course, up to you. My suggestion is to be truthful in all information you do include. At the same time, respect concerns of family members. You want your book to bring the family closer together as they share a pride in their common heritage. In other words, be open to

personal circumstances and keep your own counsel with confidences shared with you.

Adding your narrative to a genealogical chart of who begat whom brings life to these listings. Your story will answer the questions: Who were these people? What did they do? How did they arrive in this country or locale? What beliefs and attitudes do they share with family members today?

You will probably find most of your material from family members. Other places to look for information and insight include:

- Marriage licenses
- Birth certificates
- Passports/Visas
- Last Will and Testaments (This is a good place to find what a person considered important. For example, Aunt Inez may have had little money or property, but left her best dress to a niece and a brooch to a daughter. Or Uncle Harry may have left the shotgun his father gave him to his nephew.
- Poll tax receipts
- Pictures, dolls, military items, furniture—all give a sense of the person
- Military Records

(Chapter 6 gives a more detailed list of usual and unusual sources of information.)

Pre-orders are important. In some instances, heads of family in the oldest living generation receive complimentary copies. They, in turn, may purchase copies for their children and so forth. Relatives contacted throughout the research are invited to order copies. These pre-sales will help defray printing costs.

Set the publication date to coincide with a family reunion, if possible. Invite relatives to share a display of items from their individual family to add to the spirit of the event. Provide a way to order your book in advance to be delivered at the reunion. Also have books available for purchase.

You may want to present a copy to the local historical society and local library. Family members may scatter over the years, but a permanent copy will remain at these institutions for future researchers.

Working with a committee

If you are asked to work with a committee on your book— museum staff or volunteers, organizational leaders, or family members—settle various function(s) for group members from the beginning. A clear picture of each person's responsibilities will avoid conflict, save time, and made the experience more enjoyable for everyone—especially you, the writer. Consider the following tips for positive committee action:

- The committee as a whole is a good place to brainstorm ideas. Some committee functions might be: help determine topics to cover, establish a price (if there is one), find suitable pictures or documents, and serve other helpful tasks. Ask the committee's input as to the person(s) to whom the book will be dedicated and which person should write the Foreword.

- Members may assist in collecting photographs or interviewing people for the book. Request that they also get signed release forms and document their work. (See Appendix)

- Identify the committee person(s) who has editorial approval and factual control. If you are put in a position of gaining clearance for everything you write from the entire committee, the process could take longer than you wish to devote to it.

- Handle controversial topics within the committee. For instance, records might be unclear about the founding person for the organization/group or the date of establishment. A

controversial leader may have been fired. Most situations can be resolved without conflict. However, confidentiality for these discussions is important so emotions aren't stirred outside the group.

- With your input, the committee should establish a budget and approve, in advance, any additional expenditure. Keep your expense receipts and a log of your time.

- Another committee responsibility might be to plan a celebration in honor of the book's publication. You may already be approaching an upcoming major milestone for your town, church or organization that will be included in the book. Local media coverage will bring greater visibility.

- Committee members could assist in setting up book signings

- The book might be "unveiled" at a special ceremony and copies made available for sale. Many people may want to purchase books as gifts. (Always ask a person buying your book if they want it signed to them or to another person. Ask if there is a special message they want included.)

- Give the committee members plenty of credit for their participation. Volunteers often do not receive the recognition they deserve. The Acknowledgments page is a good place to permanently record their involvement. A personal as well as a public "thank you" is appreciated.

The remainder of this book provides an overall step-by-step writing guide to complete your project.

CHAPTER 3
Plan the Book

A parallel organizational plan is needed for the two major parts of your project—the book, and you. Let's begin with your schedule. Estimate a rough time span to accomplish each step of the project—research, interviews, visual collection (write captions and credit lines), write (edit, edit), publish, and market your book. If you are working with a publisher, your deadline for completion is probably already set, so you'll need to work backward from that date. However, a schedule and deadlines are just as important if you self-publish. Mark each milestone on a calendar or use a daily schedule and project chart to keep the work moving (See Appendix).

Set your work schedule

First, know yourself. I'm a morning person—so the earlier in the day I begin writing, the more I accomplish. Another writer may only be able to work in the evening after children are in bed and the house quiets down. After work or weekends may be your best time. The important thing is to designate blocks of time you can devote to working on your book.

One of the hardest accomplishments for many writers is staying on target—and staying at their computer. If you have a daily word count, keep writing until you meet your quota. Otherwise, several days may go by without coming any closer to the end of the book. You can lose your rhythm if too much time elapses between writing sessions. Writing and meeting a word count every day keep the story fresh in your mind.

> **A project that languishes under your bed or in a closet collecting dust runs the risk of staying there.**

I encourage you to set a schedule that works for your lifestyle and stick as close to it as you can—knowing that life happens and you can't always control circumstances.

Your well-developed plan, consistently followed, will prevent losing time and money. For instance, knowing all the areas of

information you need to research at each location will make best use of your time while there. Glean all you can from one site including getting release and donor permission forms signed (See Appendix). A repeat trip eats into your schedule and budget.

You next need to organize your book. The following suggestions will help you define the scope of your book—time period, special events, and people you'll cover.

Start with a timeline

Your first organizational step is to develop a timeline that spans the period your book will cover. Neither you, nor later the reader, should have to stop and ask directions. The timeline will naturally define chapter breaks from which you can estimate word count to help with scheduling. You may revise your plan as you go along, but time allotments for each chapter will help you stay on task.

Make your timeline entries brief and easy to follow. (See Appendix) I refer to my timeline many times during the course of writing a book and post it in easy view from the computer for quick and frequent reference. You may also want to include the timeline in an appendix as an aid to readers, but this is optional.

If appropriate to your story, include census figures for added prospective. These population figures help show the increase and decline of industry, effects of war or drought, and other growth/decline trends in your area. Unusual weather or occurrences in nature should also be included.

The Timechart History of America, [Barnes & Noble by arrangement with Worth Press, Ltd., 2003], or similar resource, provides a selection of parallel events throughout American history. Happenings outside your story may have helped shape that history and give your story added perspective.

As with fiction writing, start with action if you can—the moment a main event occurs such as a devastating earthquake or assassination. You can work the back story into your book as you go along. However, the timeline will help keep you and the reader in touch with the actual sequence of events.

For instance, one of my books, *Rogers: The Town the Frisco Built* begins long before the town incorporated in 1881. American Indians camped along nearby creeks, Civil War maneuvers crisscrossed the land, the Butterfield Overland Stage stopped there, lumber mills and other industries were started—all before the first railroad through the area brought about incorporation of the town. Use back story like this to add richness to your story.

Develop an expanded outline

Your timeline creates a natural outline for the book. Chapter breaks will become evident and help keep the length and word count balanced.

This rough chapter outline will include major blocks of time, events, or phases in the story you plan to cover. With this in place, expand the outline to include additional points for each chapter.

Writing flows more smoothly when you decide in advance what you want to say and the order in which you want to say it. Nonfiction is easier to write when you have a working outline. This doesn't mean that copy won't get moved around as you go along, but you have a basic idea of what will be included.

From the expanded outline, you can readily tell if you are devoting too much space to one area or shortchanging another. There should be some balance to your chapters; however, prehistory for your town, or the early childhood years of a person you are featuring, may not warrant the same amount of attention as more significant events.

Set word count

This is a good time to assign an approximate word count for each chapter. From this number, you can estimate the total words for your book. Your publisher may set a word count for you. Or cost of printing may impact on the length of a book you self-publish. Try to determine the word count/size of book before you get too deeply into your project.

Set daily writing goals necessary to meet the word count you set for finishing a rough draft of your book on schedule.

List chapter needs

When you've finished your outline, make a brief needs list for each chapter. (See Appendix.) Note people to interview, photographs to take or documents to find, sites to visit, research trips, list of research areas—and, in general, all that needs to be done to complete each chapter.

Information is rarely gathered in the order chapters come in a book. When you have finished the needs list by chapter, further organize those needs by research location to save you backtracking for information. When you are in a research room fifty miles from home, you want to get all the information you can for chapters throughout the book. You can sort the material by individual chapters when you return to your workspace.

As mentioned in Chapter 1, a book is often arranged in the chronological order in which events took place. This is a logical way to approach your work. However some local or regional history books may follow a thematic order instead. In other words, one chapter might include early churches to the present, another follows the economic growth from early businesses to today's thriving metropolis, the progression of education from the one-room school house to the multiple-grade-level schools in the current system.

This thematic approach may be easier to write in some instances. All one subject matter is confined to a single chapter rather than dispersed throughout the book as changes evolve through the years. The downside is losing a parallel movement in history of related events as they happen during the same time period. You'll need to decide which approach fits your topic best. Your publisher's guidelines may specify an approach.

Pre-story and post-story sections

The story is, of course, the most important part of your book. But it is not the entire book. Pre-story and post-story sections may be brief or extensive based on the subject and your own personal preference. Your publisher may determine the extent of these sections, but some material is always appropriate.

The sequence of beginning pages may differ somewhat but basically contain the following information. If your book is produced by a publisher, you will only need to start with the Dedication page.

Note: All right-hand pages have odd numbers.

The following incorporates additional information for the self-publisher in setting up a page layout. Just skip the parts that don't apply to your project.

Pre-story Pages

Cover	Displays the title and author(s) name. A subhead may be added to further explain the title. Use a clearly-read font with attractive colors, and eye-catching graphic.
Title page	Appears on the first right hand page and restates the title

Title should be readable from six feet away—usually the distance from reader-to-shelf in a bookstore.

Second page	May be blank or used for a list of previously published books by the author. A picture or map is appropriate for a history book.
Third page	Restates the title, author, and publisher/location
Fourth page	Copyright, ISBN, Library of Congress information, specific information relevant to the publishing and ownership of the book
Dedication	Brief description of a person or persons important to you or to the story. Picture optional.
Acknowledgments	List of people instrumental in a special way with your book—such as local museum, library, school, or town staff. This is also a good place to mention other authors who have heavily contributed to the preservation of factual information helpful to your book. Don't overlook church/organization/family members if they were involved.
Introduction	Your place, as the author, to discuss what motivated you to write the book, special connections you may have to this period in history, or unusual experiences you had researching the book.

| Foreword | Space for a guest writer—perhaps the director of the local museum or a person involved in preservation of this history |
| Table of Contents | List chapter titles. May include sub-sections within each chapter. |

Post-story pages

Various topics are appropriate to an appendix. Here are a few examples.

Appendix 1	Timeline covering the scope of your story
Appendix 2	Names and dates in office of various town officials—mayor, city marshals, fire chiefs, police chiefs, school superintendents—people who often work long hours without comparable appreciation
Bibliography	List of major works used for research. Serves as a guide for readers to pursue the subject in more detail
Index	List of important people, places, events and the corresponding page numbers.
About the author	Short blurb about you\including a photograph—material may also be used on the back cover copy or flyleaf.

Back cover	Strong promotional copy. Endorsements from notables in your field can strengthen this page and the salability of the book.

Sample layout

If you find it difficult to visualize your book, a layout sheet is helpful. It is easier for me to write to space. If you work with a predetermined page length or word count, you can more easily track your progress.

The sample layout (See Appendix) indicates all the pages in a 64-page book. Your book will probably be much longer. Adapt sheets to fit your page count. Indicate the size and placement of photographs, graphics, maps, or documents. Remember to begin all chapters and odd-numbered pages on the right.

CHAPTER 4

Establish a Workable System

You can write your book almost any place. Working efficiently and effectively just any place may be another matter. Some writers need complete quiet and even close the curtains in their offices to block out distractions. Others take a laptop to a coffee shop and write amid a background of multiple sounds including music. I compose in my office, but edit better at a coffee shop. Well, you get the idea. In most circumstances, you can control your workplace and find an environment where you are most productive.

The next step is to organize your space. Fiction writers may carry most of their plot in their creative minds. However, for a nonfiction book—research materials, books, photographs, and interview notes tend to grow overnight. The sheer volume of stuff can be overwhelming without a system to keep it in order. This chapter provides workable solutions for these issues.

Maximize limited office space

Let's start with a home office. Office is a term I use lightly. My first book dominated our dining room table for over six months and both living room couches gave up their normal use for the last two months of final work.

The first luxury in any office is to have enough flat surfaces to spread out your work and leave it there for the duration of the project. A guest room might fit the bill. I tried a separate downtown office for a while, but found I got more work done at home. Whatever I needed was always in the other space. Plus, I like to be able to work at any time of day or middle of the night and keeping all material in one place seems more convenient.

I converted a spare bedroom into my office. Closets hold four-drawer filing cabinets, a two-drawer filing cabinet extends my desk, and bookcases hold research and writing books. An L-shaped computer desk is ample for my monitor, laptop, and three printers.

Inboxes

The very nature of writing history creates paper, newspaper clippings, notes, photographs, and all the files related to the publisher, legal papers, release forms and so forth. You'll prob-ably collect three or four times the research material and visu-als you will actually use in your book.

> **If you run out of room horizontally, go vertical.**

I use filing cabinets and out-of-sight places for storage of for-mer books and materials for future stories. However, I like to *see* all the material that I'm working with on a current project. I use labeled, clear plastic inboxes—a separate box for each chapter of the book including the pre-story and post-story sec-tions. Individual boxes are also designated for the publisher, marketing ideas, earlier/edited copies of the manuscript, interviews, releases and so forth. You can stack inboxes on book-shelves or purchase interlocking shelving units at a building supply store to hold your inboxes.

> **Keep all edited versions of the book with the date of revisions for future reference. These can be tossed once the book is published.**

Rarely will you find material in the exact order you will use it. Something of interest for several different chapters will come to light in one visit to the library or in an interview covering the span of several years. Marketing ideas and mailing lists will filter in as you work. When you return to the office—sort materials, contact names, and photographs into the correct chapter box.

Using this system, what you need to write Chapter 8, for example, is ready for you in its own box—just pull the box and start writing. I've found this system helps keep my workspace less cluttered because just the materials I need at hand are neatly stacked in its own inbox.

Three-ring binders

An alternative method that I use—sometimes in conjunction with my inbox system—is keeping material organized in three-ring binders. It is easier to handle a large number of pages in order that way. This system is especially helpful if you give copies of the manuscript to a museum director or other qualified editor to read for comment. I keep these edited versions along with my own edited copies until well after the book is published. Date all edited versions—even your own—so you won't have to shuffle versions looking for the latest changes.

Later when you get galleys (printed sheets for editing) from the publisher or printer to proofread, you may need to refer to these first edits as you make final changes on your book.

Another use for a large notebook is to hold copies of photographs you've collected for the book. You will probably acquire many more pictures than will actually appear in the book. Organize hard copies by chapter with a cover sheet including the caption, donor, approved credit line, and signed release form for each photograph. You may want to include additional information for each as caption space may be limited. Keep these photographs in acid-free plastic sheets for protection and easy access. Of course, all can be kept on computer files or CD's. I like to always have a duplicate hard copy so I can see all the material at once. This is especially helpful in placing pictures throughout the text.

> **Your photo notebook can later become a good marketing tool. When you are a guest speaker or working a book signing, an open book of old pictures is irresistible and a good ice-breaker with potential buyers.**

Three-hole punched holders for business cards provide a convenient way to keep important contact information you've made while researching and writing your book. Keep the business card of librarians, museum personnel, media people, and/or vendors. These may also be people you need to thank for their involvement after the book is published. Add them to your direct mail or email contact list as potential buyers once the book is published.

Throughout the process, I also create a large binder as a Master File for the book. It includes a section for correspondence, release forms, publisher information (or printing if self-published), final copy of the manuscript, marketing plan, budget/expenditures/income, and so forth.

Work environment

Your workspace needs to be as uncluttered an environment as possible to provide space for your computer, printer, telephone/cell phone, FAX capabilities, and camera equipment suitable to your work.

Good lighting is important.

I try to keep general reference books close at hand—dictionary, thesaurus, book of well-known quotations, style manual, and information dealing with copyright and legal publishing issues. How-to books for authors and magazines for writers may offer helpful tips. Books on related state and local histories are great for fact checking and general reference.

Try to keep plenty of computer paper on hand, at least one extra printer cartridge, extra film/battery for your cameras, memory stick and other needs for a digital camera. I keep desk essentials close at hand: pens, pencils, file folders, sticky notes, tape, stapler, rulers and so forth. A daily planning calendar keeps me on track plus a wall calendar with deadlines is in easy view of my computer.

At the beginning of a new book, I start a computer file for each chapter and section of the book. I find this makes it easier to note changes and move copy around. At the completion of the final edited version, I complete one copy with page numbers on a single file and disc.

Take your office on the road

I've retraced my steps too many times because I didn't have what I needed with me on location or neglected to get complete information on site. If your book requires out-of-town research trips, it may be worthwhile setting up a small travel office in your car. A large box should hold most of your material. Items you might want to include based on your equipment are:

On the Road Office

- Extra copies of all forms—photo/property release forms and lists for follow up
- Laptop/printer/paper
- Extra discs
- Extra printer cartridges (for portable printers)
- Cell phone with car and room charger
- Tape recorder that allows you to pause when transcribing
- Tapes
- Labels for tapes/discs
- Flash drive
- Professional camera (take a throw-away camera too—just in case)
- Business cards
- Stapler, tape, sticky notes, magic markers, pens, pencils
- Notebook
- List of email addresses—phone and fax numbers (keep a copy on your laptop)
- Maps/directions for your trip
- Bug spray if you plan to tramp around outdoors
- Sturdy shoes/jacket/umbrella/hat (see above)
- Bottled water/snacks
- Flashlight
- Any necessary medications in case you stay longer than expected
- Other essentials for overnight stay

The Scout adage, "Be prepared," applies here. Checking off the items on your various lists is like a pat on the back for a job well done. More importantly, items will be on hand when you need them. Things to do will get done.

Forms and Records

Writing is a business. You will be a happier and perhaps a more profitable writer if you keep your records current, accurate, and complete. All writers have probably fumbled through sticky notes or searched for handwritten scribbles jotted on backs of envelopes, often losing important information along the way. Some people enjoy working that way and, if you're one, use the system that works for you.

Some forms are necessary to document your work. Adapt sample forms from the Appendix. Below are suggested forms you will need to create (or use the samples in the Appendix), document, and keep track of a range of information. Tailor forms to fit your specific project.

- Release forms. Includes releases to use photographs, oral interviews, documents. or other material—actually, for any item not in the public domain
- Interview forms – these forms help remind you to get all critical information while you are on site
- Research documentation
- Expense forms
- Mileage forms
- To-do items
- Call – call return list
- Thank-you reminders
- Forms for any other activity you need to track

Expenses

Establish your systems as part of your pre-planning so you don't overlook necessary information you will later need for documenting your project. Expenditures can be easily overlooked. For instance, I'm always surprised at how

many miles I travel while researching a new book. Keep a running travel log of your mileage and related expenses.

Even small costs for making copies add up. You may find making copies of original material, newspaper articles, letters, and so forth give a more reliable support to your work than relying on handwritten notes alone. Making your own copies allows you to underline or highlight the most pertinent material. Try color coding your markers to the subject matter—green for marketing ideas, blue for leading citizens, yellow for other notables, orange for events, and so forth. You can then more easily find notes for each broad subject area.

You may be able to negotiate a deal with the local historical society or museum to help keep costs down when duplicating their files or photographs. Offer to supply copy paper or to pay their cost for making copies.

If a local camera shop makes all your reproduction pictures, you might ask the manager for a discount on your work. If they comply, be sure to mention them on your Acknowledgments page.

Keep a record of all your expenses and income on your computer or use an accounting book from your office supply store. If you keep a running total of expenses by category throughout the year—your expense record will be ready at year's end and organized for your tax return. I staple all receipts together by category as an organized back-up if I ever need to show documentation.

I keep records for several years. I do this for legal purposes. Also when I write books in the future, it is good to look back and see how I fared on past projects. You can use these numbers to analyze your spending habits throughout the project—where did you spend the most and the least amount of money? Are there places where you can cut costs on the next book?

For most writers, money is spent before publication and before royalty or sales income begins. Draft as realistic a budget as possible at the beginning of the project to serve as a guide.

If you are under contract with a publisher, read the contract thoroughly before signing. Don't hesitate to call the editor and ask questions. Some publishers pay an advance against future sales to help cover some of the research costs in writing the book. This is not always the case, especially for smaller press runs for books of mostly local interest.

CHAPTER 5

Find Your Comfort Zone
--and the Help You Need

On hearing that you are writing a book, well-meaning friends or colleagues may say, "I'd love to help you write your book." Pause. Think about it. Then respond.

This chapter suggests advantages and disadvantages to writing solo or with co-authors to help you can decide which arrangement is the best choice for you. Suggestions for protecting your time are also offered regardless of which writing approach you choose.

If you feel comfortable handling the research, writing, photography, and marketing— working alone may be the best route for you. Control of all aspects of the book is in your hands.

Or, if you know someone more experienced in at least one or more aspects of the project, you might consider a partner or multiple partners.

If the book is your idea, take your time in deciding to go it alone or join forces with others. Consider the following ideas to help make the best decision for you—and the book.

Write with co-authors

> "Partners" is *not* used as a legal term in this discussion. Check with your attorney about possible ramifications of a legal partnership.

I have written both solo and with co-writers. On my first book, *The Old Burying Ground, Beaufort, North Carolina*, I worked with two partners—Diane Hardy, a photographer, and Mamré Wilson, a researcher. The photographer was very talented, had a dark room, and could shoot and print many of the pictures. The researcher had a credible reputation in the field and was already collecting material about the subject. Fortunately, we had ready access to old photographs and historical documents.

We each were responsible for producing our individual part of the process. The three of us had worked together several times on other projects, so when I suggested the book, all fell into place.

In concert with the other partners, my primary role in the collaboration included: contact with the publisher, organizing the contents, selecting some subjects for photography, setting the schedule, page layout, and the actual writing of copy based on the research provided. I helped keep track of signed releases for all material including visuals for the book. We held regular meetings to discuss progress and plan the next step. Even though our roles were well defined and different, we were each involved with every aspect of the book.

Take the decision to choose a partner(s) seriously. Trust is an important element. You need to be comfortable that the people you work with are accurate in their research and correctly document all information. You won't have time to double-check each other's work.

Co-authors can make or break a project and personality is a key factor. For instance, a controlling, precise personality does not mix well with a person who is careless with details or deadlines. Yet, some opposing strengths may help create a good balance.

Address pertinent questions up front. Here are a few questions worth asking. How well do you each work with others? Does the potential partner have comparable time to devote to the book? Does each partner have sufficient financial resources to pay their share of the expenses? Are they equally visible and credible in the community? This could be an important factor later in book sales. Will each partner be responsible and have the skills needed for the follow-up marketing phase? Or if not, do they have comparable or trade-off skills to support the project?

I suggest that you create and sign a simple Letter of Agreement defining the individual roles for each co-author. (See Appendix) Below are points from my experience that you may wish to consider. Add other items to fit your project. Some decisions will need to be made by everyone in the group. Others need only be shared with two or more persons. Check with your attorney or accountant for legal advice on all matters.

Consider the following areas and adapt an agreement to your own situation:

Areas For Co-Author Agreement

1. Define the project (approximate answers)
   - Subject/time period covered by the book
   - Length of book
   - Number of visuals
   - Chapter topics
   - Pre- and post-sections (dedication, acknowledgments, index)
   - Budget
   - Schedule /deadlines/progress reports

2. Negotiate the role/responsibility of each author (Some may be shared efforts)
   - Research
   - Interviews
   - Collecting visuals
   - Photography
   - Writing
   - Editing
   - Fact checking/proofreading
   - Document procurement
   - Contact with potential publisher or printer if you self-publish
   - Contract negotiation
   - Financial record keeping

3. Establish procedure for:
   - Certifying source credibility
   - Approving expenditures
   - Setting deadlines
   - Selecting a publisher or printer
   - Resolving conflicts

4. Determine legal aspects
   - Copyright ownership (Who owns the book?)
   - Order of author names on the book cover

- Decision for future reprints
- Applying for tax ID numbers
- Reporting and paying taxes
- Shared royalties
- Reimbursement for expenses (or establish an equitable *quid pro quo*)
- Confidentiality
- Monitor liability potential

5. Assign spokesperson(s) for the book
- Media contact
- Book signings
- Speaking engagements

6. Agree on a consistent system to document research, get signed release forms, keep expense receipts and reimbursements current, monitor contract with the publishers, and handle other specified management details

7. Agree on regular meeting times and agendas

This may seem like a long list but, the more you consider *before* you start working together, the smoother and more professional your relationship will be. Most importantly, select compatible as well as capable people to work with you. If you have never worked with the potential co-author, check with someone you trust who has shared a project with him or her. *Talking big* and *performing well* are not always synonymous.

My experience working with other creative people was excellent. However, I would discourage working with a full committee if avoidable—even from the museum, library, or historical society. (See Chapter 2 for tips on working with a committee) These are usually lovely, dedicated, and knowledgeable people, but waiting for group agreement to proceed with your work is tedious. Too much input can weaken a book—perhaps even bring the project to a halt over disagreements or internal politics.

> The best reason I've found for working with a partner is that he or she shares ideas, brings additional and needed skills to the table, inspires you when you're down, and helps keep the project on schedule.

Keep your meeting times enjoyable and low key. On my book cited earlier, we three co-authors usually met for lunch on the waterfront, discussed our recent work, and planned the next phase. I believe that the key to this success was respect for each individual's area(s) of expertise. The book has enjoyed reprints and continues to sell.

Write solo

My experience with partners fit a closely defined project very well. However, in general, my personal preference is to write solo and make the final decisions. I find it difficult to keep the tone and approach consistent when working with another writer especially on a long narrative. I like the independence of selecting the parameters for the book, identifying people to

interview, making selections for the visuals—and most of all, setting my own schedule. If I wake up on a Saturday morning in the mood to visit a site included in the book, I haven't the patience to wait until next Wednesday when another writer can go too.

I work best in the early morning but, if the words are flowing well, I may still be writing late into the night. Depending on the role of partners, schedules may not fit. I also like to have all research materials in one place when I need them for easy reference. This may not be possible in a shared project.

Unlike fiction, where characters can sometime take on an energy and life of their own, nonfiction characters are tied to truth. This does not mean that your words can't breathe life into their actions. But how well you identify with your characters and the hardships or challenges they faced, determines your ability to bring them to the reader as real flesh and blood people. You might find it difficult to share the same insight into a character with another writer who has a different viewpoint.

There is not a right or wrong way to work. My suggestion is to know yourself and any potential partner well. The match can be as wonderful as the partnership I experienced, or a disaster. Time spent researching and writing a book should be mostly exciting and energizing. You want the experience to be positive for each person involved. Choose the method that is most productive and satisfying for you.

Protect your time

Whether you work solo or with others, wise use of your time is of utmost importance. Set aside a specific time for your writing and respect it. This will help you and others understand its importance. Let family and friends know your schedule. It is easy to be pulled away from your writing for lunch, golf, shopping, fishing, or doing the laundry—whatever. Allot time for these activities outside of your writing schedule. Eventually others will begin to understand and respect your space.

Of course, life happens and some flexibility has to be expected. But when you get a call to join a friend for the morning, say, "Sorry, I'm working until two today. How about meeting later?"

Having a daily schedule as well as a project schedule helps keep you to track. (See Appendix) I'm usually up at 6 am and in my office by 8 am. I work until lunch and then pick up the mail, exercise at the gym, and stop for coffee. This gives me a break and the coffee keeps me going in the afternoon. If the creative juices begin to run low, I use that time to update my blog, handle correspondence, check email, do research, or handle other activities that keep me moving.

The variables in your life will dictate your daily schedule to some degree. Young children at home, a full-time job, and other considerations play a role in your plans. What's important is choosing a way that works, and works as consistently as possible for you. The key to success is staying at your computer or yellow pad for the prescribed time. Nothing will get written if you're jumping up every few minutes to do something else.

> **Stay with the project even when it's not going well. It *will* get better.**

The work you did in Chapter 3 gave you an approximate number of chapters and a projected word count for the book. Set up a rough schedule for your story before you agree to a deadline for the completed project. Each book is different. Research materials may be close at hand for one book, or considerable travel may be required for another. Estimate time needed for research, interviewing, and collecting visuals. Leave the bulk of the time for actual writing. You may need extra days at the end for additional research, finding that last picture, editing, rewriting, and editing one more time. Pre-story and post-story pages may take longer than you expect—especially the index. Chapter 8 walks you through the mop-up needed to prepare the final manuscript and visuals for the publisher or printer and sending them out on time.

> The expression, "double the projected time and triple the projected expenses" may have some truth to it.

Join a writers' group

If possible, find a writers' group in your area. Time spent with other writers discussing both your work and their work is usually time well spent.

A good critique group can serve as a resource for your writing. There are as many different approaches as there are writing groups. However, every group has one thing in common—improving each writer's work.

Members usually present portions of their work for review by others. According to the expertise of each, work is discussed in light of correct grammar/punctuation, interest and clarity

of copy, consistency of the author's voice, and logic in the order of presentation. Fiction and nonfiction are critiqued differently according to the requirements of each genre.

More participation is available in small groups, but you hear a wider variety of comments on your work in larger groups. Find what works for you.

Certain unwritten rules are usually observed in these groups. "Say something good about a work first, and then make suggestions for improvement" is a good rule to follow. In my writing group, the person whose work is being critiqued holds a large sponge to emphasize that the author's role is not to argue with the critique, but to *absorb* what is being said. The author is under no obligation to make the changes, but should take them under consideration especially if more than one member makes the same suggestion.

Comments are not aimed at the writer, but at the work. You may need to toughen your sensitivity if you are used to family/friends saying that everything you write is, "Wonderful." Writing that is "wonderful" is not necessarily publishable. So listen, learn, and then follow your instincts.

Attend writers' conferences

Writers' conferences serve the same function as a writing group, except on a larger scale. Professional and successful authors lead workshops on various topics to help participants do a better job of writing and be more successful at publishing, if that is the goal.

Time is often available to meet one-on-one with book and magazine publishers, editors, and agents to discuss your work. These time slots are coveted and usually limited to about ten minutes. If your work is ready to submit, take advantage of these opportunities. The 25-word blurb that you wrote for Chapter 1 will help you refine your *pitch* to the time allocated.

Attending a writers' conference for the first time is an eye-opener for many beginning writers. Just go, and learn. As you become more advanced as a writer, use the conference to make contacts and, hopefully, come away with an opportunity to submit your work to an editor or agent.

CHAPTER 6

Research Sources:
Leave No Stone Unturned

Explore family histories

You may be like many writers who developed an interest in history from hearing family stories. (See Chapter 2) I remember spending Sunday afternoons as a child listening to visiting relatives tell "remember when" tales that only got better with the retelling. Turn over that first research stone with family members—yours or those of others—who will have these kinds of memories and would love to see their stories preserved in your book for future generations.

The blurb on the back of my second history book, *Rogers: The Town the Frisco Built*, listed me as an "author and historian."

My first reaction was that I am a writer and author, yes, but historian! I hadn't thought of that. Webster defines a historian as a "writer of history." So, as writers of history, we can each claim that title.

As a historian, your first effort may be to collect related family history by interviewing family members about their memories of your hometown or region. Collect letters, diaries, photographs, and other artifacts that may still be in the attic, on the family farm, or in a trunk in your sister's garage.

Your book may not be about your family only, but also include people who helped build your town, owned the mills, ran the stores, organized churches, made laws, sold tickets for the train, went to war in Germany or Iraq, or kept the home fires burning through hard times and good. A good place to begin your research is with those in the community who can recall (or have access to) these supporting stories.

Museums and historical societies

The next major resource will probably be the local museum or historical society. You'll find like-minded people who love history and respect your desire to preserve it. If the museum or society has more than one staff person, ask to speak to the director. Your professional courtesy should develop a positive rapport. Other staff may be in charge of displays, photographs and documents, or the archives. In smaller museums and societies, a volunteer president may be in charge of all of this.

The museum director will probably know if other books have been written on your subject—or if a new one is in progress. The museum support for your book is important. Tell the director about your project and what you hope to accomplish. Your timeline and 25-word summary will show the scope of your book.

The staff will probably be delighted to help you with this project. Small museums are too often understaffed and overworked. They may welcome someone else to compile a history of the area. The director can show you museum documents—files, books, recorded oral interviews, artifacts, and photo files. Ask about maps, other publications, programs, or special newspaper editions celebrating a significant town anniversary or event.

The museum director may also be very helpful in checking the names of people and events you plan to include in your book. He or she can easily spot an omitted person or family who made important contributions or exerted great influence on the history of the town or region.

Obviously, you cannot include every name. However the more names you do mention, the more people will have a personal interest in reading and purchasing your book.

Members of long-standing in a church or other organization should be able to also supply those names or know the best person to contact for that information.

Relationship with the museum staff

Rules and regulations differ from museum to museum. In some research rooms, you can go through file folders at your leisure; in others, staff will bring requested folders to you. This is a little frustrating—as you may not know what to ask for until you have browsed through the material. Staff may also provide white gloves for you to wear to protect original documents from unseen and harmful oil from bare hands during handling.

The person in charge of photographs may remain in the room as you go through the files. Don't take offense. The rules are for everyone. As a historian, you share their desire to protect valuable documents.

You may be able to borrow photographs for reproduction. Some museums can reproduce in-house or arrange for reproductions for you. You may be allowed to take photographs of artifacts on display. Check in advance for the equipment you will need to compensate for special lighting or glare from glass cases.

Whatever methods you use for obtaining visuals or other requested information, get a release form signed/dated while you are on site (See Appendix). Retracing your steps for a forgotten signature or release form wastes valuable time. Occasionally, permission from an outside donor may be necessary to use these materials. The museum staff will help obtain this permission for you. Double-check correct wording for the caption and donor acknowledgment.

Follow the format of your chosen stylebook as you take notes. (See Appendix) This procedure saves considerable time later on as you complete your book's documentation. When you get ready to write the bibliography, your source listings will already be in the correct format.

Be appreciative of staff time. Requesting extensive help from museum staff at a time when a large group of fourth graders is on tour doesn't make for a congenial working relationship. Arrange in advance for access to records, available photographs, or other materials you need. Also ask for permission to make copies of research documents. I keep a package of copy paper in my car office for this purpose, and offer to use my own paper. You may still need to pay for use of the machine if you have a lot of copies.

Ask the director for a list of the most important people or families that should be included in your book. You might also ask a knowledgeable staff member to read select portions or the entire manuscript and check for omissions or inaccuracies. Clear this with the director in advance. Always acknowledge these people in your book and send thank-you notes. I've also found that a basket of chocolate candy for the staff is appreciated.

If a staff member does agree to read and fact-check your manuscript, present only a few chapters at a time. Specify an agreed upon deadline for its return. Don't leave your request until the last minute.

When you've accumulated all the information you can from the various museums, be sure to ask for suggestions of other sources.

Other usual and unusual sources

Local librarians or Special Collections librarians at a nearby university or regional library can be a fruitful source for material. People who inhabit these musty areas, are thrilled to share their knowledge—so don't feel hesitant to approach them and ask questions. Some of this information may be obtained through the internet or on official websites. Also consider the following sources for information:

Sources

- County courthouse records (land records, arrest records, tax records)
- Registrar of Voters
- Genealogical records
- Files at historic sites or battlegrounds
- National associations or organizational archives that

specialize in your area of research
- Literary works and films that reference your subject or region
- Shipping records/ship's manifests (passenger names/date/port of entry)
- National archives
- State and national park records
- Archives from corporations and non-profit organizations
- Corps of Engineers (maps, pictures, documents of waterways, dams, bridges)
- Minutes of past meetings for city, county, and state offices
- Architectural firms
- Church and denominational groups
- National Register of Historic Places records
- Event programs
- DAR (Daughters of the American Revolution)
- School yearbooks and alumni records
- Military service records
- Funeral homes/burial/cemetery records
- Cemetery headstones
- Chamber of Commerce (Main Street office if the city has one)
- Newspaper morgues (past issues)
- Census Bureau
- Local photographers

Many towns had an early photography studio or a special person who took lots of pictures you can examine. In my hometown, Gary Townzen—a third-generation barber on First Street— collects early pictures to use in his annual calendar of historic downtown. So, ask around.

Identifying the people and events in old photographs can be tricky, but with some digging on your part, most of the essential information can be found. Try to get as much complete information as you can from the person supplying the visual— names of people, where they are, what they're doing, and the approximate date the picture was taken. If the person making the identifications is not authorized to grant the release, find out who is and contact that person.

Newspaper microfiche might be housed in the local library or in the morgue (place where out-of-date copies are kept) at the local newspaper office. You may be lucky enough to find original newspaper copies still in existence. Find out the access process. Ask about special issues of the paper that may have been published in celebration of city milestones or special events. These issues are often a rich deposit of information and may include reprints of even older newspaper articles. Make sure that the information is correct and doesn't just repeat an earlier error.

End every conversation with a source by asking, "Do you know another person to interview who may have family histories, photographs, or documents to share."

Ensconced in the hush of a research room filled with dusty files and fascinating stories, it is hard to keep on the subject without pursuing one side story after another. If you cannot let one of these stories go, make a note where you found the information and add it to your file labeled "Future Projects."

> **A word of caution. As the saying goes, "No one who loves to read can clean an attic." Research may be so much fun that it becomes an excuse for not sitting down and writing your book.**

Keep the level and amount of research in proportion to the project. For instance, if you are writing an article or small booklet for the historical society, keep the research in line with your space. Of course, a full-length book requires much more material. In any case, you will probably accumulate more information than will appear in your publication. But the depth of knowledge is apparent even though all details may not be specifically listed.

Successful interviews

Face-to-face interviews with people, who share a passion for your subject, is one of the most satisfying methods of research. When you make an appointment with the person(s) you plan to interview, let him/her know in advance the kind of material you are interested in obtaining. This doesn't limit the subject but will help establish a comfort level.

The interview setting should fit the situation you've planned—video, tape recorder, or simple note taking. Most interviews may just be you and the subject, but interviewing multiple people at once can also be successful. Here are some tips for both types of interviews.

Individual interviews

First person accounts from people who were present during the time covered by your book are the most interesting. But also stories handed down from family-member-to-family-member carry their own authenticity. Exciting stories can come up unexpect-

edly during an interview. An elderly person may tell you that he or she doesn't remember very much anymore. But when you start to show pictures or copies of old newspaper articles from a past era, the person may start to laugh and tell the most wonderful tale unobtainable by any other means.

You may be comfortable taping interviews, but always carry a notebook. The notebook is a good place to jot down the correct spelling of names, take side notes, or to remind yourself of other questions to ask that may occur to you during the interview. However you record the session, know your equipment so you aren't fumbling with it while you are trying to put the person at ease. This reminder applies to video equipment as well. Working with a partner or a museum volunteer who has technical expertise, can free you to concentrate on the interview.

Learn as much as you can in advance about the person you plan to interview. You don't want to ask an obvious question about something you should already know.

Develop questions that build on each other rather than jumping from one topic to another. Start with non-threatening questions and gradually build to more personal or controversial ones as your subject relaxes and begins to trust you.

Take an informal picture of your interview subject for your own records. You may also want a more professional picture to use in the book, local press release, or spin-off magazine or newspaper article. Be sure to get a release for the picture and for the interview for possible future use. Do not promise the person that either the interview or the pictures will be used. Your editor will probably have the last word on this.

Date all interviews using a consistent format to record the person's name, place of interview, and main topic of conversation. (See Appendix) At the end of the interview, read quotes aloud if needed to verify their accuracy.

Make note of anything said in the interview that begins with, "Don't use this in your book, but...." Take the quote, but *don't* use the information unless you are given permission to do so. If you feel the level of trust is good, consider asking before you leave about using the confidential story. If you're lucky, the person may just say, "Oh, go ahead and use it."

One more obvious reminder about equipment—take back-ups for any equipment you are using. Chapter 4 offered suggestions on how to organize your on-the-road office so you aren't caught without the equipment you need.

If the interview subject asks to see your coverage of them before it is published, be diplomatic, but make it clear that you don't show your final copy in advance of publication. Most publishers follow this policy to avoid impinging on the integrity of the publication. However, if you are dealing with a controversial or sensitive subject, read back your subject's comments/quotes while you are still together. If you find later, while checking your notes that you still have a question, call them back for verification.

Again, always ask if that person has pictures or other memorabilia that hasn't been discussed. And does your source know anyone else who would be good to interview about the subject.

Group interviews

Sometimes more information can be obtained from interviewing two or more people together. They will spark each other's

memories and, before you know it, they may forget you're there and just get lost in the storytelling. The "remember when" syndrome kicks in pretty fast.

Video taping interviews is a good idea especially when interviewing more than one person at a time. It can be hard to distinguish one voice from another when you later review voice-only tapes days after the event.

The local historical society might set this up as a program, especially if they are conducting an oral history project. I've had great success with this as one story leads to another. Once a group of fisherman, we interviewed for a local historical society, told their stories of life on the water and soon started singing sea chanteys used while pulling in their nets. Our video caught this priceless bit of history.

People may wander off topic onto unrelated subjects. You may need to bring them back to the subject during an interview. Guide gently. Don't be too hasty to break in. You might find out something that you didn't even know to ask. Play it by ear.

Again, don't forget to get a picture of each participant or a group shot, signed releases for the interview and pictures you take or they provide.

Now, go out and start turning over those stones. Look for nuggets of history gold!

CHAPTER 7

Be Professional
Be Interesting

People featured in your book may have lived hundreds of years ago, but your job is to make their hardships, triumphs, and failures real to the reader through your words and images. These images complete the story told through genealogical records or other documentation.

Your writer's voice

You have your own distinctive voice as you write. The expression, "That sounds just like John or Suzanne!" is a good indication of what voice means. Some people write and speak in short, brief sentences. Others create long, flowing sentences full of color and emotion. Noticing the pace, flow, and harmony of words in other books can help you find your own voice. Keep your voice consistent throughout your book. Readers relax and settle into your rhythm.

Rules are important

Your story needs to hold the attention of the reader. Stumbling over misspelled words or incorrect grammar breaks the flow and interrupts the concentration of the reader. A good reference book on composition will provide the rules for grammar and punctuation that give polish and professionalism to your writing. Or ask someone knowledgeable in this area to check your work. Communication with the reader is more successful when you follow the customary form and manner of writing. You care about this because your goal is to communicate with your reader. And your publisher cares.

In addition to writing correctly, publishers also want you to follow the same style consistently. Stylebooks such as the following are well-known guides for writers:

- *The Chicago Manual of Style*
- *The Elements of Style*
- *New York Times Manual of Style and Usage*
- *Associated Press Stylebook*
- *The Wall Street Journal Guide to Business Style & Usage*

Many publishers specify their preference for the stylebook used by their authors. Following a guide throughout your writing will help answer any questions you may have about correct usage.

Guides are particularly helpful in keeping the format consistent for footnotes and the bibliography. It pays to study these rules in advance. You will save considerable time if you document your source notes in the correct format as you gather information. (See Appendix)

If you are self-publishing, the choice of stylebook is up to you. I find *The Chicago Manual of Style* published by The University of Chicago Press to be user-friendly.

Creative nonfiction techniques

The growing popularity of creative nonfiction places greater demands on the author to write nonfiction in a more lively way. *Creative nonfiction* seems to be a contradiction in terms. However, it does not mean to *make up history*. The term simply means that the writing skills used to bring life to fiction may also be applied with success to nonfiction. You've probably heard a child in school moan, "History is so-o-o boring!" Well, as you know, it needn't be so.

Unlike characters in a novel, the people you write about are or were real flesh and blood. Their exciting lives, true tears, and rollicking laughter make up the stuff of history. Look for their wants, needs, and dreams. What obstacles did they overcome and how did they achieve their goal? Who had the most to gain or lose? In other words, *find the story.*

The historian's job is to breathe life into the people who appear in his or her book. Passions can become fiery through words from a letter to a lover or actions inspired from angry words in a political speech. The reader gets to know a character through the personal dialogue and stories he has told or are told about him. The reader needs to feel the heat of battle or experience a weary cowboy's lot as he slumps in his saddle on a long cat-tle drive to Kansas City. Sounds and smells also add realism.

One example of an entertaining glimpse into life in the 1800s might be found in the town ordinances passed by the first civic leaders. Laws in my hometown during that period prohibited spitting on floors of businesses, throwing wooden or vegetable substance on buildings, singing indecent songs, slaughtering animals within the city limits unless they were "rabid"—all giving insight into how people lived at that time.

Other examples might include stories of death and horror on home soil during the Civil War often told in first person through early letters or diaries preserved in family trunks. Or tell the story of the town banker who was caught with just the change in his pocket when the stock market crashed, or how families "made do" during the Depression. Make your point-of-view character(s) come to life. Every town or region has its own story of happiness and sadness.

Your story will be more lively if you keep paragraphs reasonably short. Intersperse short sentences with long ones. Use a conversational tone and style in your writing. Find strong verbs to substitute for was and were. Write as if you are telling the story to a small group of people sitting around a campfire with you. For instance, instead of writing, "She was happy," say "Her eyes twinkled and her face broke into a smile." Captivate them with your word pictures.

Most of all, tailor your copy to your audience. You decided at the beginning whether to write your book for children or adults. If writing for children, know the appropriate vocabulary and what level of detail is acceptable for your targeted age group. An adult audience may be general or scholarly, and the vocabulary should be chosen accordingly. Regardless of age or level of interest, be accurate.

Site visits

Visit the site where your story takes place if possible. Stroll down the sidewalks. Note the character of the houses and gardens, feel the cool shade along tree-lined streets. If you're writing about a battle, set the scene for your readers by picturing young soldiers charging down a hill followed by their officers on horseback; smell the sulfur of guns just fired; hear the clash of swords, and the cries of the wounded. Make it real.

For instance, in the Battle of Pea Ridge in Arkansas, a family—whose home was confiscated for a field hospital—huddled in their basement while blood from the dying dripped through the floorboards onto their heads. First-hand accounts like this from those who were there at the time, plus your own acute sense of the conflict, will bring the story to life for the reader.

Include major weather events in your timeline and in your story. Were the winters harsh? Did waves of humidity rise from the bayou during summer? What kind of clothes did the people wear during the era you cover? What customs surrounded birth, marriage, or death? Describe the women's mourning clothes. What kitchen or farm implements were used? Crops grown? What games did the children play?

Visuals for your story

Descriptive words alone do not tell the whole story. The stern expression and stiff posture of great, great, grandfather and mother are best shown in a tintype, photograph, or even a painting or drawing to add to your text. The old saying that "a picture is worth a 1,000 words" was as true in the past as it is today.

Through various visuals, your reader can see a church on fire, faces of proud young soldiers leaning out a train window blowing their last kiss to a sweetheart, shoppers filling the town streets on a busy Saturday shopping day, a small child throwing corn to a yard filled with baby chicks, or a group of men lined up in front of the local hardware store discussing the business of the day.

You will probably be amazed at how many photographs you'll find. The museum should have volumes of pictures and be able to give you names of people in town who have many more. Keep the number of images you collect relevant to the scope of your book. Be considerate of your time and others—be very specific about subject and time frame for material you request.

You will need the following for the pictures or other documents you use:

- Printable quality
- Description of the picture—names of the people, approximate year, event, and anything else that identifies it. This information will go in the caption.
- Credit line information. For example, "Photo donated by Jerry Jones" or "Courtesy of the Rogers Historical Museum."
- Signed photo release (See Appendix)

The same procedure will apply to maps, copies of letters, diaries, documents, or artifacts you include in your book.

Technology in digital cameras and computer software is progressing rapidly. Your needs for appropriate equipment will vary depending on your project. If you need to shoot close-ups of small museum artifacts, displays behind glass, ruins at a distance, written documents, or replicate existing photographs—you will need specific equipment.

A good relationship with a camera shop may save you time and money. If you don't already have equipment that fills your needs, talk to a reliable person at the shop—perhaps the manager. My experience has been that experienced staff will have unlimited patience showing you what they feel will work for you. Be sure to explain the project and how the equipment will be used. Many shops also offer classes.

Your publisher or printer will have guidelines for visual submissions. Follow these guidelines. If you have questions, call or email the appropriate person on their staff.

Carefully handle material on loan to you and keep the items for as brief a period of time as possible. You shouldn't need to send original material to the publisher—and never do so without permission from the lender. Thank each person for his or her contribution and stress that *not* all material may be used in the book. That final decision will probably be the publisher's based on space and cost. You don't want to raise expectations and then disappoint your donor.

List on the Release Form that you are asking for permission to use their material in the book, on the cover, in press releases, or related magazine and newspaper articles, or in any other promotion for the book including electronic. If you are dealing with a professional photographer and are paying him or her for photos, you may be held to *one-time-use-only*. In that case, you may need another release and possibly pay a fee for each additional use of the photograph.

Some publishers place all the photographs in a separate section of the book—front, back, or middle of the book. I find it more interesting to intersperse visuals throughout the copy. Either way is appropriate and gives greater credence to your story.

CHAPTER 8
Seek a Publisher or Self-Publish

Okay, you've decided on the subject for your book and selected an eye-catching, interest-grabbing title. You have a grasp of the major events you want to cover through your timeline and you've researched the competition. The next step is to decide how you hope your book will be published—by a national publishing house, university press, or local historical society. You may, based on your own resources and ability to market the book, decide to self-publish.

Your choice may depend on your own finances, time, and talent as well as the nature of the book. If it has limited focus and audience, self-publishing or working under the umbrella of a local historical association may be in order. If your book has statewide, regional, or even national implications, you may seek a university press or a large publishing house.

Research potential publishers

Reference books such as *Writer's Market* published by *Writers Digest Books or Writer's Guide to Book Editors, Publishers, and Lit-*

erary Agents published by Prima Publishing are among the various resources for writers seeking a publisher or agent. These guides give detailed information about the industry. Check your library or bookstore for a current copy to determine its usefulness for you. These books are expensive to purchase for a one-time use.

You will find lists of publishers and—in some cases, agents—, the type of books they handle, submission guidelines, royalties offered, and often tips on how to impress them with your work. You will have a better chance of acceptance by approaching publishers that specialize in history or a specific time in history. Check the internet for the most current information about your selections.

Publishing is a serious business and new projects are carefully judged for potential success. Rejection is often part of the process for various reasons—perhaps your book doesn't fit the publisher's mix of books or they have recently published a book on your subject. Don't be discouraged by rejection. One writer's group even gives an award for any writer who receives his/her 100th rejection letter. Why? Because it indicates the level of commitment on the part of the author, and being turned down is part of the game.

Submission guidelines will specify the approach a writer should take. Some require a query letter only. A full proposal goes beyond the letter and may also include a chapter outline, book synopsis, author biography, and one or two sample chapters. (Outlined later in this chapter) Just send the material they want in the manner in which they request—email, hard copy, CD and so forth. Be sure to address the query letter to the correct editor.

Once accepted by a publisher, you will be working with an editor and a publicist who know the business and know what sells. You will have access to their professional editing and advice on the scope of your project.

The publisher handles the cost of printing and some of the publicity expenses. They determine the percentage break for bookstores selling your book as well as your royalty rate on the finished product. Their contract specifies the entire working relationship, including deadlines, manuscript specifications, rights they are buying, number of copies for the first printing, number of free copies to the author, and the price break for author-purchased copies.

The publisher also arranges distribution of your book and accepts unsold or damaged copies—important considerations when you approach a chain bookstore to carry your book or to set up a book signing. Read your contract carefully and fully understand what rights you are selling. Seek legal advice if you have any questions or are unsure of what is acceptable in this business.

Take time to examine books already in print that seem similar to the book you are writing. Note the copyright date and check the publisher. Note the number of chapters and approximate word count for each book. Local or regional history books usually are not as lengthy as those for a national or international market.

A university press often publishes books not carried by larger main-stream publishers. They may have a higher interest in manuscripts based on the mission of their institution and/or regional history. Find out how many books they publish each year.

Small presses are another option. They don't have the budget or perhaps the marketing reach of the larger publishers but may be more open to your book idea. Again, research the market. For very little money or sometimes at no cost, you can order a catalog of books from a company on your list. Their most current books will probably be listed on the internet. You can readily see if they have published a book similar to yours.

Knowledge of the usual criteria requested by publishers will help you plan your book. Here are some facts about potential publishers you will find in the resources mentioned earlier:

Find Facts About Potential Publishers

- Number of manuscripts a publisher receives each year that are agented, unagented, or from first-time authors—as well as the percentage in each category
- Submissions accepted only through an agent
- Types of fiction and nonfiction they prefer
- Total number of manuscripts published each year
- Rights purchased
- Word count accepted
- Length of time to respond to your query
- Criteria and format for all visuals
- List of recently published titles
- Percentage of royalty to author—and the basis on which the royalty is determined
- Advance offered, if any
- Additional tips to receive positive attention to your proposal
- Correct name of editor to receive your material
- Reminder to include a SASE (self-addressed stamped envelope) for the return of hard copy submissions, if rejected

Pitch your book

As mentioned earlier, some publishers will only want a query letter rather than a full proposal. In that case, you may have to wait (often months) for them to reject or request further material based on your query.

Use your letterhead for the query (easily created on your computer). Follow the standard business letter format. Single space the query letter with a double space between paragraphs. (Double space most other components of a full proposal.)

Include as much of the following information in your one-page letter as possible. If the publisher requests a full proposal in their guidelines or after they receive your query letter – use any or all of the other components listed under *Proposal Package.*

Query Letter

- This one-page cover letter is your chance to convey your enthusiasm for the subject and sell the publisher on you and the book. The letter should include the title and subtitle of your book. Express your passion for the subject, the depth of your research, special qualifications you hold as a writer on this subject, and how your book differs from any competing books.

  Point out the need for the book and its value to the reader. For example, there may be a major town celebration in two years with a six-month long series of activities culminating in a big three-day event expected to draw 250,000 people. The book has the support of the local historical museum and town library and will be promoted in their programs and later sold in the museum bookstore.
- Briefly describe your reason for writing the book
- Detail any personal connections you have with the subject—perhaps you are the great, great, grandson or daughter of the founding person of your town. Or note if you have journal notes by the featured individual or founders of an organization or town.
- List other related works you have published.
- Mention if you are including original research in the form of a diary or other documents—or have a wealth of photographs, maps, or other visuals.

- Note if the governor of your state or other notable has agreed to write the foreword or a supporting blurb for the back cover of the book.
- Make a strong case for the part you are willing and capable of contributing to marketing your book. Also state whether this book is to be the first in a series of books you are planning, each reinforcing the sale of the others.
- Mention that chapter outlines/full proposal package is available.

Complete proposal package

Publishers expect a proposal to be submitted in a professional manner. Use high quality white paper, black ink, and standard margins of one inch on all four sides of an 8 ½" x 11" bond paper.

A nonfiction book proposal is different from the approach used for selling a novel. A novel is usually finished before seeking a publisher, but a nonfiction book should appear to be open to suggestions from the publisher. This doesn't mean that the book is not already written but that there is room for further input.

Here are the usual components of a full proposal to a potential publisher that includes your query letter:

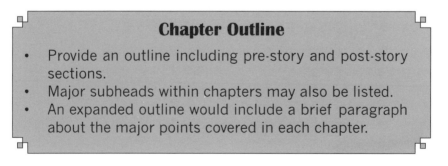

Chapter Outline

- Provide an outline including pre-story and post-story sections.
- Major subheads within chapters may also be listed.
- An expanded outline would include a brief paragraph about the major points covered in each chapter.

Synopsis

- Summarizes the book pointing out major highlights, usually between one and five pages—expand on topics covered in your query letter.

Author Biography

- Write in the third person, in paragraph form, single spaced.
- A complete resumé is not necessary unless it is relevant to your writing or ability to promote the book. Do list information about yourself that establishes you as a credible writer and special reasons why you are the person to write this book.
- List writing credits.
- Publishers are interested in the platform a writer has to help promote the book. You may already have a following from previous books. List your membership in related professional organizations, experience in public speaking at workshops/seminars, radio, or television. Give past experience at book signings. List your successful blogs or websites.

Market Analysis

- If you are writing a local/regional history, give the population of the general area. List every venue for possible sales: large and small bookstores, retail stores that might carry the book, annual events where large numbers gather especially if there is a history theme, alumni meetings, historical and genealogical societies, and so forth.
- Note mailing lists and media contacts you have. Indicate your willingness to produce a direct mail campaign and pursue various members of the media.

- Analyze competing books. Note the copyright dates, slant of books that differ from yours, and so forth. Without criticizing other work, set your book apart from the competition and show ways in which your book fills a need that will lead to sales.

A projected word count and date of completion is helpful. In calculating completion date, don't cut yourself short on time. Allow a few weeks for mop up—double check details, get a late interview, and so forth. Better to err on the side of more time than less—and have to request an extension.

Find out your publisher's needs if you can. He or she may be trying to meet the schedule for a holiday catalog or some other deadline. If feasible, it may help to assure the publisher you can work within his deadline. Making his or her life easier is appreciated.

Thank the editor for considering your book and state that you look forward to a reply requesting the complete manuscript.

Self-publishing

Securing a contract with a standard publisher can often be a lengthy process. Competition is keen. As stated before, there are advantages and disadvantages to any method you choose for producing your book.

If you want control over the entire project and do not take editing suggestions easily, you may prefer to self-publish. Or you may have a pressing deadline when your book needs to be finished. In any case, carefully consider the following responsibilities you may have to self-publish:

- Money needed in advance for production and marketing
- Editing, page layout, selecting visuals, and fact checking
- Distribution (Major bookstores usually only accept books handled by a distributor who will take returned, unsold, or damaged copies of books) Distributors take a cut for their work and it is your responsibility to establish a working relationship with a credible distributor.
- Applying for and purchasing ISBN numbers, bar code, arranging copyright, and adding Library of Congress information
- Handling your own marketing (Granted, you will be an active participant in the marketing of a successful book even if you go with a publisher.)
- Legal ramifications are yours to research and bear responsibility
- You will determine the credibility of your book in the marketplace

Consider joining Publishers Marketing Association (PMA), *www. pma-online.org*, a national organization for small publishers. Another is the Small Publishers Association of North America (SPAN). These organizations—and others—can be a valuable resource in learning the skills necessary for small press publishing or self-publishing.

Read your contract with a self-publishing house or printer. Some self-publishing houses take on many of the publishing responsibilities and pay you a royalty on the books. You may have to pay for editing and other services offered by these companies. Be sure these additional services are not ones that you could handle yourself or get done at a lower cost elsewhere. Read the fine print and discuss with your attorney.

If you work directly with a printer, consider the following:

- Cover stock: weight, coated/uncoated, no-curl lamination
- Text stock: weight, size, brightness
- Ink: Black & white, black plus a color, 4- color (might only use on cover)
- Binding: Perfect (glued), saddle-stitched, comb binding
- Cost for visuals
- Design costs if needed
- Estimates on press runs: 500, 1,000, 5,000 copies
- Method of packing/delivery
- Storage – does the printer offer climate-controlled storage –cost for storage
- Shipping/handling costs. Does the printer drop ship directly to your customers or do all books come to you for handling and shipping? Cost of these services.
- Payment method

Holding your own book with your name on the cover is a thrill. However, especially if your book is self-published, take one last pause when you receive copies from the printer or self-publishing house before celebrating and sending your relatives a copy.

Open a couple of boxes and check the copies. Yes, even under the best circumstances, page order may be out of sequence or a section of pages left out completely. So check. If you work directly with a printer, be sure you are getting what you paid for before handing over the final payment. This double-checking can be done in a friendly way and, if the printer is professional, he/she will handle your problem depending upon the extent of the mistake.

CHAPTER 9

Down the Home Stretch

Before sending your manuscript to a publisher or printer, make a final check to ensure that your work is as error-free as possible, all work documented, release forms signed, and budget is in order. Feel confident that you have offered your best work and are ready for publication.

Double check the *to-do* lists

Builders keep a punch list of items to be corrected, checked, finalized and so forth before a job is declared finished. Sometimes they are waiting for a part to come in, a subcontractor to complete their portion of the job, or a mistake to be corrected.

Writers use similar punch lists. The lists you kept throughout the process of writing the book now need to be checked for unfinished items. You may be waiting to confirm a date or spelling, or to find out if a story—that's too good not to tell—is true. The expression, "Never let the truth stand in the way of a good story" doesn't apply to history—unless its lack of authenticity is noted.

After your contract is signed and you have sent your manuscript to the publisher, the publisher will send you galleys to proofread. Make minor changes and add pre-story and post-story sections if not already completed. Familiarize yourself with standard editing marks. If you don't know them, check your stylebook for this list.

A suggested punch list will remind you to check the following:
- Completed release forms
- Biographical information
- Captions for accuracy
- Recheck galleys from the publisher to be sure that captions match visuals and that pictures have not been "flopped" making the picture backward. If possible, people in a picture should face toward the spine, rather than off the edge.
- Check timeline dates with chapter copy for agreement
- Add last minute material to finalize the copy
- Recheck source copy for dates/names

Final Edit

The galleys are not the place to make major changes in your story and start moving chunks of copy around. Minor changes should be made without charge from the publisher or printer, but major Author Alterations may cost you.

Let your copy sit for a few days after you've made all the changes. Then read one last time. Don't over edit, but add improvements where needed. After you've made changes, re-read the entire paragraph to ensure the flow is still smooth and that nouns and verbs still agree.

Completed pages will come next with visuals in place and editing changes made. Captions for visuals are a likely place for a mistake, so check these carefully. Be sure that one page reads correctly to the next and the correct chapter follows each previous chapter. Go over information in the pre- and post-pages. This may seem strange, but check book title and chapter titles. You've looked at these so many times, you may only be seeing what you think you see.

Page numbers for Index items are completed last as editing changes may move information to a different page. Topics can only be correctly indexed upon final page completion.

Return the final copy to the printer/publisher by the date requested. Spend some of your time waiting for your books to arrive by finishing your *to-do* list.

Thank-you notes

Showing appreciation is an important part of the overall process. I doubt a history book was ever written without the author receiving some information from other people or sources. If you are the organized type, you wrote your thank-you notes as you went along (to be mailed after the book is published). If not, now is a good time to do this. Hold notes for those you plan to accompany with a copy of your signed book.

Don't return materials too soon

Keep all photographs, documents, written material such as letters and diaries, books, and other material on loan to you until the book is published and you have checked each final printed page for accuracy.

Your *to-do* list will come in handy again where names and addresses for borrowed items/donors will be listed. Return material in the condition in which you received it. If material was not used, express your appreciation for the opportunity to present it to the publisher.

At book signings, pictures used and those not used in the book can be displayed. People will often stop by your table to look through these pictures from the past.

Leave files organized

Even while I'm hard at work on my current book, I'm already itching to start the research on the next one. However, my experience is that you need to get all of one project organized and put away before starting a new one.

Files may be kept by subject matter or by chapter. Filing by subject matter may be the best way if you plan additional work or spin-off articles covering this same period of time. Filing by chapter works better for me. If a question arises or I want more information about a particular subject, I go to the chapter file and all the material and copies of visuals are there.

As mentioned earlier, you may wish to keep a master file in a large three-ring binder (4 1/2" or larger) for written material and photographs collected whether you used them in the book or not. Correspondence with the publisher, release forms, and so forth are also kept there. I eventually empty my organized inboxes and all the material goes into a research file, master file, or photograph file.

You will need work space and access to much of this information during the marketing phase of the book that is discussed

in the next chapter. But finish the project. Don't leave ends dangling to aggravate you in the coming months when you are deep into your next exciting project.

CHAPTER 10

Promote Yourself
Promote Your Book

Your proposal to the publisher detailed the size of your potential market, avenues for selling your book, and ways in which you would personally assist in its promotion. Now is the time to make good on these assertions. (Marketing information in this chapter deals primarily with books published for sale to the general public. Emphasis on marketing to a church, organization, or family members can be found in Chapter 2.)

You're proud of your book, enthusiastic about sharing it with others, and have made the commitment to do your part to ensure sales. Marketing is the part of the process where you finally interact with your readers—first through publicity and then face-to-face at book signings and speaking engagements. If you are self-published, the responsibility is mostly yours to set up the venues and make the sales. Even working through a publishing house, a large part of the marketing success rests with you.

This task may seem awesome at first. It's not. Just be yourself and talk about what you know. You'll find help along the way from people in the media who do this every day and will usually lead you through interviews. Although you may not feel confident at first, you will soon play the game with ease.

Develop a marketing plan

Do your homework well. The following ideas will help you successfully market your book. The word "marketing" simply refers to the umbrella under which you find each of the following promotional strategies. As with any successful venture, you need a plan. Know what your publisher has scheduled before setting up your own means of promotion beyond the publisher's assistance.

Your plan may include additional press releases, interviews, direct mail, book signings, speaking engagements, and the development of other promotional materials to market the book. Add a website or blog hyping your book. Organize your overall schedule so that each effort is timed to support the others. For example, announce an upcoming book signing during a radio interview.

Even if you work with a publisher, you should be able to find opportunities to sell copies of the book you have purchased at "author's cost" from the publisher. For instance, if you give a talk to the local historical society or library in their conference room, you can set up back-of-the-room sales. Remember you are responsible for collecting and paying sales tax on books you sell yourself. Know your own state law and the laws of other states you may visit to sell. Check with your attorney or accountant.

Primary and secondary markets

Most authors work within a limited amount of time and money available for the promotion of their book. Therefore, it is important to know your market—who they are, where they can be reached, and the message that will fit their interests or needs.

Your primary audience may be members or supporters of the local museum, library, genealogical association, cemetery preservation group, Main Street members, high school alumni groups, former businesspeople—the list goes on. Fortunately, these potential buyers can be reached through events, newsletters, or programs they sponsor. Direct mail is more productive to lists of these well-defined groups.

Other highly motivated buyers may be the general public, long-standing families in the area or newcomers interested in knowing more about their new home. These groups will be interested in coming to book signings and for programs you lead on the subject.

Schools and libraries may be secondary markets. Secondary markets are more cost-effectively reached through radio, TV, website, and print media. Direct mail is too scattered to be a good vehicle for general promotions.

Press Releases

A current and complete media list is important. Develop your list by checking local and regional newspapers and magazines for the person responsible for writing book reviews and feature articles. Call area organizations and ask for their newsletter editor, especially those that deal with your subject area. Contact the talk show host for local radio and TV stations. Become familiar with the format, interests, and style of the media you approach. Their articles and interviews provide free publicity for your book.

A general release should go to these outlets—area newspapers, magazines, newsletters, historical societies, museums, libraries, book stores, and appropriate retail shops.

Press kit

Determine which media people warrant just a press release/book cover and those who will receive a complete press kit including a copy of your book. Build your media packet with the following items tailored to your contact and your book:

Press Kit

- Press release
- Suggest reasons their audience/readership would be interested in the book
- Fact sheet (with little known amusing or intriguing facts)
- Brochure or flyer on the book
- Your personal vita/picture
- Copy of the book cover (send books to the most likely media to respond)
- Statement of your availability for an interview
- Q&A page(s) is helpful to your interviewer
- Add sticky notes, marking pages in the book with interesting stories or visuals.
- Include all contact information about you and places where books can be purchased.

Writing the release

Write the press release on your letterhead labeled PRESS RELEASE. Include contact information with your name, address, telephone, email, and website. (Set up a website if you don't have one and, if possible, link it to the town's website and historic sites/organizations in your state.) Under the letterhead, write FOR IMMEDIATE RELEASE and date above the copy. Include the items listed above. Send a complete packet to the most important or most likely media to cover your story. A trimmed down version can be sent to media less likely to carry your story.

The release should be written in third person similar to a newspaper article—who, what, when, where, and why in the lead. Give an interesting overview of your book with a couple of your best anecdotes or quotes. Tell something about yourself and why you wrote the book. Try to get a quote from a museum director or well-known local writer supporting the book. Describe your book as a *must read*.

I suggest you use a post office box and cell phone for business contacts, keeping personal information private.

Give-away books

You will need to give books to selected members of the media. Cost can add up quickly for books you purchase, even at the author's discount. Send books only to the media/book reviewers most likely to promote your book. Send a book cover to the rest of the list. Your publisher or printer should be able to supply you with covers and bookmarks.

You'll probably give a book to close family members, local museum and library, mayor's office, Chamber of Commerce or downtown Main Street office, and maybe to a couple of very venerable members of the community. However, if you give copies away to the people most likely to purchase one, who is going to buy it? Naturally, you want everyone to have a copy of your book—former high school teachers, classmates, friends, church members, friends of friends, relatives and so forth. Keep in mind that you will receive very few free copies from the publisher and beyond those, you pay.

Friends and other writers may say during the process of your writing, "I want a copy of your book when it is finished!" Try not to answer, "I'll see to it that you get a copy." Instead tell them you'd love to sign one for them and will let them know when you are having a signing—or the most tactful words you can manage. They may not be aware that a publisher only gives the author a limited number of free copies.

Media Interviews

As you prepare for your media interview, anticipate questions in advance. To whatever question you are asked, include the points you feel need to be highlighted in your answer. Subtlety is the key here. You should be able to work your points in smoothly without being abrasive.

Interviews with the press can take place anywhere convenient—their office, your office (if not at home), in a coffee shop, or at the museum—sometimes over the phone. Remember to give your fact or Q&A sheet to the interviewer plus a copy of the book and picture of you. Interviewers may wish to take a picture of you holding the book or in a setting to their liking.

Have talking points in mind. Be sure to mention where and when the book will be available. For radio interviews, have talking notes, dates, quotes, and so forth on a card for quick reference. TV interviewers seem to have notes, but their subjects usually just hold the book. Ask if the studio would like pictures from the book for your interview and, of course, have a copy of the book to show. Give a copy of your book (signed if they like) to the host.

Understand the world in which the media live. Newspaper and magazine writers may have the space for your article changed at the last minute. If there is a major breaking story when you are being interviewed, your time may be cut short or rescheduled. Be understanding and accommodate their world.

Send the writer or interviewer a thank-you note following your meeting or when the story appears. Establish a good relationship. You will need to contact the media again to cover your book signings, workshops, speaking engagements, and to cover the publication of your next book.

Use Direct Mail

Email or announcements on your website are by far the least expensive method of reaching your potential audience. You will need to set up a PayPal account or other means of handling payments for your book. Customers can, of course, send you a check. But every extra step a person must take in order to purchase lessens the chance they will take action.

A successful direct mail program depends on a good list, compelling copy, easily-understood information, and a detachable coupon to return with a check or credit card acceptance. A picture of the cover of the book is essential and may be used on the inside and on the mailer side of your flyer.

Budgets can range from modest for a simple flyer to a higher cost for a more extravagant, four-color brochure printed on heavy glossy stock. Keep in mind the budget you set in the beginning. A plain sheet of good quality white paper with black ink, creatively written and designed, can be as informative as four-color—but may not attract as much attention.

The most important aspect of direct mail is the list. Your lists may consist of local people who are interested in your subject. Look at your primary and secondary markets and determine if direct mail is appropriate for your book and for your audience. You may wish to test the validity of your lists by first mailing to a select number of names. If the response is good, than mail to the entire list.

Do not address your mailing piece to "resident." If you are writing a book about your hometown or local region, high school alumni lists can be good. Lists beginning with the 50s graduating classes forward may be your best markets. If you have a thousand or more graduating seniors in each class, you may want to hand pick names you feel most likely to respond.

Other lists might include members of the Chamber of Commerce, civic groups, CEOs of area businesses, churches, women's organizations, historical associations (including battlefields, historic districts, house museums, cemetery preservations groups, DAR and so forth), teachers, elected leaders, and city employees. Some of these lists may easily be obtained from a member.

Be creative, but watch the budget on your direct mail piece. If you use outside services to create your flyer, there will be cost for design, copy writing, printing (2-side), color ink if you use it (color might be important for the cover picture of your book), labels (ones you print yourself or those you purchase), tabs, and postage. You can create your own flyer on the computer. Add pictures or other visuals.

If you use a printer, ask them to pre-fold your flyer into thirds if you are using an 8 1/2 x 11 sheet. All you then need to do is affix the label, add postage and close with a tab. Use live stamps if possible. The recipient feels the mail is more personal with a real stamp rather than a printed indicia. Perforated, transparent tabs for the fold work best to hold the piece together during mailing. The flyer won't tear apart when the recipient pushes through this kind of tab.

Copy

Make your copy interesting and intriguing—in hard copy or electronically—so the potential reader can't wait to buy your book. The second part is providing a coupon that gives you and the buyer all the information needed. Here are some copy suggestions:

- "JUST RELEASED" gives a sense of immediacy to the piece
- Picture and name of the book in large, well-set type
- Briefly tell what the book covers (use some of your back cover promotional copy)
- Note humorous or sad details
- Encourage readers to reminisce about the good old days
- Suggest readers personalize the book by adding their own family history
- Keep it concise with enough white space to be reader friendly

For the coupon

- State the name of the book and price
- Give space for name, address, city, state, zip, telephone, email
- Allow space for mailing information for gift copies
- Number of copies @$ price of book
- Sales tax per copy @ $ per book (in state)
  (Check sales tax laws with your accountant or attorney)
- Shipping costs (Offer a discount for multiple orders)
- Place for amount enclosed/check number/credit card information (if you have an arrangement with your bank)
- Ask if they want their book signed (yes or no)

You might enclose a bookmark with your book as a little gift to your buyer. A bookmark is easily made on your computer. You and the buyer *will* be happy if you mail books—*and* deposit the buyer's checks promptly.

Mailing the book

To cover your mailing costs, total the postage and the cost of a padded envelope to protect your book during mailing. Make a sample envelope with a full-size dummy book. The post office can then advise you on the best method of mailing, taking time and cost into consideration. A writer friend of mine suggests a more economical method. She first wraps her books in recycled foam sheets from a local furniture store, and then mails the book in a plain manila envelope. Lighter, less costly—and protected.

Sales Tax

If your state collects sales tax, you will need to set up a sales tax number for any books that you personally sell. Report and pay all state sales tax collected. *Check with your accountant or attorney about in-state and out-of-state requirements or any other legal questions you may have.* Laws may differ from state to state. If you sell your book direct to bookstores or retail establishments, you will need to get their resale number.

Your publisher handles sales tax for the books they sell. They sell books to you minus the tax and you sign a form agreeing to collect tax on any copies you sell. *Don't* compete by undercutting the publisher's sale price.

Record keeping

Set up a system for tracking book orders that works for you. Consider keeping the customer's return envelope, order coupon, and copy of the buyer's check. Record the date you mailed the book to your customer. You will also need to keep both your total sales for each month as well as the sales that include tax for reporting. Check with your accountant or attorney on specific requirements for your state.

Keep your mailing receipts. These can add up very quickly. As can your mileage back and forth to the post office.

Schedule book signings

Media interviews and other aspects of the marketing plan may seem difficult. However, book signings are one of the easiest ways to bring attention to your book. If you go through a publisher, he/she may arrange some of these; however, it is up to you to arrange peripheral signings and to schedule repeat signings at chain outlets. Hopefully, your publicist will contact the retail stores and book outlets you suggest. You don't want the events spaced too closely together, but you do want to take advantage of the excitement that a new book creates.

Plan your events to coincide with other scheduled events. If asked to speak to an out-of-town writer's conference, for instance, also offer to present a program at the local library, set up a book signing at a bookstore or retail shop. Contact the local/area radio or television station for an interview. Also contact the print media for an interview/article to fit this timeframe. You may not be able to plan such broad-based publicity, but try to do as much as possible or appropriate.

Many variables go into how many books are sold at signings. Success depends upon publicity (press coverage, signs and flyers in the store, and interviews with the media), in-store support, and most of all on your ability to engage customers and present an inviting backdrop for your book. Unless you are a local notable, best selling author, or celebrity, you may not sell many books at these events. But they are worth the effort for free publicity and visibility. The event may encourage subsequent sales of the books as well as those sold that day.

Here are some hints for holding a successful book signing:

Hold a Successful Book Signing

- The best situation is when the author speaks or reads short passages from his/her book with an area for people to sit and ask questions in a relaxed atmosphere

- More often the author is given a table at the entrance of the store or somewhere in the middle. If this is the set up, make it as attractive as possible. Have a number of books stacked on the table and one on a table easel.

- Stand most of the time so you will be eye-level with potential buyers. Make eye contact with people as they come in and introduce yourself. Tell them you are the author and would be happy to sign a book for them. Signed copies enhance the value of the book.

- A 18" x 22" (or smaller) poster on foam core placed on an easel works well and draws people to your table. The poster may have a color picture of the book cover, brief promotional copy, and maybe your picture (Check with your office supply store.)

- Put a bright colored cloth on the table

- Have at least 2 chairs for people who may want to carry on lengthy conversations with you. They won't block others to your table.

- Offer free book marks or post cards with a picture of the cover and other information about the book, author, price, publisher, and order blank

- You might hold a drawing at your table. Provide printed forms for name/address/phone number/email plus several pens. A large clear glass bowl or brandy snifter serve well as a receptacles. This attracts people to your table and adds to your mailing list for the next book.

Don't offer a free copy of your book as the prize. Why buy one if you might get one free?

- Props that relate to the book are also useful. If you are writing about trains, have a toy train or any items that match the book. A Victorian doll might go with that era or a vintage model plane for a WWII book. You might use these as prizes for your drawing.

- Your in-store support person should announce your presence and book signing at intervals during the time you are in the store.

- Most signings last about two hours. Try to plan the event during prime customer time in the store.

- Be sure to write a follow up thank-you note to the store manager—you want to be welcome when you plan your next book signing.

Speaking Engagements

Historical societies, churches, civic groups, school classes, and libraries are often looking for program speakers. Check whether any of these groups have an ongoing speaker series that you may join. These are usually small, informal, and friendly gatherings.

If you are invited, ask your contact if he/she is sending out a press release. If so, send them a picture of yourself, copy of the book, plus a fact sheet. There are many local newspaper and TV event calendars where your program could be announced.

These are usually free and great ways to keep your book/event visible to the public. If you are speaking to a non-profit group, you might consider making a small donation from your sales to the organization.

Ask for a podium and mike if your prefer this set up. Here again, make the setting as appealing as possible. Put a sales table near the entrance to the room in advance of the meeting. Old lace and needlepoint may be more appropriate to one book while battle or sports scenes more appealing with another book. Have two chairs, and a couple of good pens along with a stack of your books near the door. Ask for a person from the sponsoring organization to handle sales and money while you offer to sign books after the program. Bring change with you or accept only checks. Use your poster and easel.

Tailor your speech to the audience. Have a handout for every person. Your bookmark or flyer make good handouts. Be sure there is information about ordering books in the material. If you have additional speaking engagements or signings scheduled, mention them at the event.

Keep your talk lively, conversational, and humorous if appropriate. Leave time for questions and book signings. Refreshments—usually supplied by the group—help keep people around longer after the meeting.

Keep the pressure on

The publicist (from your publisher) will arrange the initial, major book signings and sales locations. However, there are other appropriate times for you to sign books. If you are self-published, these arrangements are always up to you to initiate. For instance, the local museum or historic site may have scheduled events throughout the year. Your town may be celebrating a major milestone in their history, or a reenactment might be held at a battlefield nearby—such events attract people interested in history or the past, your primary target market.

The community relations director at a national chain bookstore may be planning a signing day for local authors or a special promotion for local books on history. Ask bookstores, libraries, and relevant organizations to keep your name in mind for such events. The more you are *out there*, the more books you will sell. Keep your publisher informed of your efforts. They appreciate authors who take initiative to increase sales.

Hurrah for you!

You may feel that it has been a long journey from inception of your book idea to actually holding a published copy in your hands. I hope that the suggestions in this book have made the road less bumpy and that you have enjoyed the entire experience.

Celebrate your success. And start your next project.

APPENDIX

The following forms are for your use as you work through the process of creating a book. Adapt forms and/or create ones tailored to your specific book. The forms correspond to the chapter discussing that particular topic.

These are not meant as legal advice. Consult your attorney or accountant for advice on all legal or financial matters.

Sample forms include:

- Daily work schedule
- Timeline
- Sample layout
- Project worksheet
- Needs list by chapter
- Sample release form
- Sample co-author agreement
- Source documentation
- Image records
- Interview log
- Site visit information form
- Publisher contacts
- To-do lists
- Media contacts

Make as many copies of these forms as you need for your own use. These may not be reproduced for sale or distribution without the express consent of the publisher.

For more information: www.mhcollins.com

Daily Work Schedule

Establish a daily work schedule to ensure that deadlines are met and your work stays on course. Make copies of all relevant days for your project or use a separate calendar devoted exclusively to schedule your writing time.

Block time for research, site visits, picture taking, interviews, and writing. You will need time to edit, re-edit, and prepare your manuscript for publication.

Daily Work Schedule

Month_____ Day_____ Year _____

6 am	
7 am	
8 am	
9 am	
10 am	
11 am	
Noon	
1 pm	
2 pm	
3 pm	
4 pm	
5 pm	
6 pm	
7 pm	
8 pm	
9 pm	
10 pm	
11 pm	
Go to bed!	

Sample Layout

The sample layout is for a 64-page book with 60 numbered pages. Some chapters naturally run longer than others. If you mark the pages or sections of pages for visuals, you will have a more accurate word count estimates. Your book will probably run longer than this. Adapt the layout sheet to fit your book. Final layout will probably be determined with the publisher.

Sample Layout
(Adapt to fit your book)

Cover	Title Page	Map	Publisher Info.	Copyright	Dedication	Photo	Acknowledge-ments
					p.1	p.2	p.3
Acknowledge-ments cont. p.4	Introduction p.5	Foreword p.6	CHAPTER 1 p.7	p.8	p.9	p.10	½ Page Photo / ½ Page Photo p.11
Full Page Map p.12	CHAPTER 2 p.13	p.14	Full Page Document p.15	p.16	CHAPTER 3 p.17	p.18	¼ Pic ¼ Pic / ¼ Pic ¼ Pic
Full page pic. p.20	p.21	p.22	p.23	p.24	p.25	p.26	½ Page Photo / ¼ Pic ¼ Pic p.27
CHAPTERS AND PAGES CONTINUE.........				Appendix I p.61	Appendix II p.62	Index p.63	Last Page Blank p.64

Timeline

This timeline is a sample of selected events taken from the book *Rogers: The Town the Frisco Built* (Arcadia Publishing, 2002). The timeline in the actual book begins in 1541, almost 340 years before the town incorporated in 1881. These backstory events enriched the story and led to greater understanding of the resulting town and its successes. The county was established before the town incorporated, so county events are listed as well.

If you wrote a family narrative history or the history of an organization, events outside that more narrow focus give perspective to the lives of people and the decisions they made.

Timeline

Date	Event/Source
1839	First school opens in Benton County in the Masonic Lodge

(List sources of information as you collect it)

Date	Event/Source
1840	Arkansas population, 97,574; Benton Co., 2,228
1846	War with Mexico begins; Benton Co. men enlist at Ft. Smith
1849	First parties lead the gold rush from Ft. Smith to California
1851	Peter Van Winkle/family moves to Benton Co. and construct a mill at War Eagle
1858	Butterfield Overland Stage stops at Callahan's Tavern
1861	Arkansas secedes from the Union, joins Confederacy
1862	Confederates lose the Battle at Pea Ridge
1881	First passenger train comes to Rogers on May 10 Town of Rogers files incorporation papers in June. *Rogers Champion*, first town newspaper is published
1884	Arkansas apples win first prize at New Orleans Exposition
1886	Fire destroys many downtown buildings in Rogers
1888	First telephone lines run
1893	First hospital is established in Rogers
1895	William Jennings Bryan, 1896 Democratic Presidential nominee, speaks locally

Project Worksheet

An estimated schedule for your entire project will help you keep focused and establish a rough writing plan. This kind of planning allows you to "see" the project as a whole. Add items to fit your book.

Project Worksheet

Project title: _____

Author(s): _____

Summary (25 words): _____

Project description (book, speech, article): _____

Projected length: _____

Number of chapters: _____

Research sources: _____

Visual sources: _____

	Start date	Complete date	Research
Collecting visuals			
Writing			
Pre/post-sections written			
Rough draft complete			
Publisher contacts/queries			
Editing/final fact checking			
Final copy			
Prepare for publication or self-publish			
Other			

List of Chapter Needs

Use this form to list needs by chapter:

- Onsite visits
- Interviews
- Visuals to collect
- Other "to do" items by chapter.

Add more chapters and space to the chart as needed.

List of Chapter Needs

Chapter	Research items	Interviews	Visuals	Site Visit	Other
Pre-story sections					
Chapter 1					
Chapter 2					
Chapter 3					
Chapter 4					
Chapter 5					
Chapter 6					
Chapter 7					
Chapter 8					
Chapter 9					
Chapter 10					
Post-story sections					

Sample Release Form

Signed release forms are needed if you use photographs of people/property, or documents—or conduct interviews. A signed release is required for anything you use that is not in the public domain. The signed forms grant you and the publisher permission to use the photography/item/information from the subject or owner of items. Of course, check with your attorney for all legal advice.

Most people are happy to sign the form. If you encounter controversial items, take special care to get permission.

Sample Release Form

USE YOUR LETTERHEAD

Release Form

I hereby give permission to (your name and company) _____
_____ to use interview comments and *photographs in (name
of book) _____ published by (publisher's name)
_____. Permission is granted to use
this material in the text, cover, and other promotional venues both printed
and electronic deemed helpful to the publisher or author in the promotion
of said book.

The undersigned releases (your name and company) _____
_____ and the (publisher's name) _____
in which this material appears from any and all claims and demands aris-
ing out of or in connection with the use of this material or images.

Authorized signature _____

Date _____

Caption information _____
_____

Credit line _____
_____

* List each photograph or document you might use. Be sure to get the
caption information and the person/institution to credit with the picture.
(Example: Courtesy of the XYZ Historical Society, or Photo by Charles
Jones)

Co-Author Agreement

This sample agreement addresses a specific project. Include only items that pertain to your book. The purpose is to help the participants address all the important issues involved in working together and ensure mutual agreement in advance.

Sample Co-Author Agreement

Letter of Agreement

This agreement outlines the entire working relationship between (name of first person) _____ and (names of other people) _____ to research, write, publish, and market (name of the book) _____.

- The project description: (Changes may be made as the project progresses with agreement by each person)
  Name of project _____
  Length of project (number of pages) _____
  Black and white/color _____
  Paper size/stock of interior pages and cover _____
  Binding _____
  Number of planned visuals _____
  Possible sources for visuals _____
  Number of planned copies (if self-published) _____
  Publisher (if known) _____

- For the purpose of this agreement, each person will be responsible for the following:
  Person 1 (List all responsibilities)

  _____

  _____

  Person 2 (List all responsibilities)

  _____

  _____

- [If you are working with a publisher] The ___% royalty will be divided and paid to (person 1) and (person 2) for all copies sold through the publisher.

- Media copies and other copies for promotional purposes do not receive royalties. Net monies from copies sold directly by authors shall be divided between the two authors. Appropriate sales tax will be deducted and paid by the appropriate parties listed below.

- This constitutes the full and complete agreement between these two parties.

- I agree to all provisions of this agreement:

Agreed (Person 1)   Date
Agreed (Person 2) _____   Date

Source Documentation

Your publisher may specify a stylebook for you to follow. If not, find one that is comfortable for you to use. Follow a consistent format and document notes accordingly as you conduct your research. When you are ready to write the bibliography, your material will already be in the correct format.

I suggest using a separate sheet for each source. Make your notes on that same sheet and/or attach copies of original documents. Same idea applies if you are using your laptop.

You may have found an old newspaper article in a file at one of the museums you visited. It helps you later on to not only record the correct source information but to note where you found the file and perhaps the name of the staff person who helped you. You may need their help again.

Source Documentation

Stylebook

Subject: _____

_____

_____

Location of source(s): _____

_____

Contact person(s): _____

_____

Sources

Publications (title, author, publisher, date of publication and so forth—written to stylebook format)

_____

_____

_____

Contact person/contact information:

_____

_____

_____

Additional sources listed:

_____

_____

_____

NOTES:

_____

_____

_____

_____

_____

Image Records

Visuals make your story more interesting and relevant. You will probably collect many photographs and other visuals in the course of your research. An image record will help you keep the donor, captions, releases, and credit lines organized.

Image Records

Chapt.	Image #	Image Caption	Donor	Credit line	Release	Item Ret'd

Interview Log

Acquire complete information while you are with the interviewee and ensure all appropriate release forms are signed. As noted on other charts, document any items on loan so you know where to return material. This may seem like a needless step, but material soon begins to pile up. As you separate items into chapters, it becomes harder to keep up with the sources of loaned material.

Take a picture of the subject for your records and/or for possible use in the book.

Interview Log

Interviewee _____ Date _____
(Use additional forms for each member in a group interview)

Address _____
City _____ State _____ Zip code _____

Phone _____ Cell Phone _____
Email _____

Subject of Interview _____
_____

Interviewer _____
_____

Place of interview _____
_____

Date of interview_____
_____

Releases signed/attached (interview, property, photograph etc.)
_____

Document visuals, captions, credit lines, and so forth on the Image
_____
_____

Joint down questions that you want to ask during the interview.
_____
_____
_____
_____

USE A SEPARATE SHEET FOR NOTES

Site Visit Information Form

You gain first-hand knowledge when you visit the place(s) where your story took place. You experience—at least in part—the sights, smells, surroundings, and many other tangibles and intangibles that were part of your subject's daily life. If you're lucky, natural forests still stand and the configuration of the land remains the same. Rivers may still flow much as they did years ago. However, the passage of time or a recently built dam will have changed the way this looks today.

You should still be able to find what the topography was like from the Corps of Engineers or from early pictures/maps at the local historical society. I feel, that if possible, you need to be there to experience and know the place.

Take note of the reactions from your five senses so you can convey this reality to your reader. History comes alive as you help the reader become part of the story.

Site Visit Information Form

Site Visit

1. Site address (attach map if appropriate) _____
_____

2. Describe the part of the story that took place here _____
_____

3. Describe the setting _____
_____
_____

4. List or photograph still-existing landmarks, buildings, or natural terrain of the surroundings. Visit the local cemetery, if appropriate. Take pictures of the grave markers of your story's subjects. You may find conflicting dates of births and deaths--this is one source for authenticating the truth.
_____
_____

5. Talk to the local people. I have yet to visit a place that didn't have someone who knew what happened, was related to my subjects, or had items or writings passed down through the generations. It is worth taking time to find these people.

6. Check the source list in Chapter 6 to be sure you leave no stone unturned while you are there.

7. Make contact with the local historical society or museum, introduce yourself and briefly explain your project —in advance if possible. Ask what kinds of information and visuals they have relating to your subject. Also get a list of names/location of possible people to interview or who may have lots of photographs or a family connection. Set appointments ahead of time to make the best use of your time when visiting.

8. In some towns, the Chamber of Commerce also has historical data. Also ask if there is a Main Street program. This national organization is responsible for maintaining and preserving historic sites and structures.

9. Give everyone your business card. They may think of something at a later date and need to know how to contact you. Ask for their card, if appropriate.

10. Follow-up thank you notes are a quick way to cement a relationship and ensure future cooperation. Take the time to get the correct spelling of names/titles and contact information. You may wish to return for a book signing or to present a program once your book is published.

Publisher Contacts

You decided the audience for your book in Chapter 1—children, youth, academic, or general adult readership. If you plan to go with a publishing house or university press, you will need to research these companies to determine if your book is a good match.

Develop your proposal package to meet a publisher's guidelines. They may be different for each publisher. You may have developed an inside track with a publisher or spoken to one at a writers' conference who gave you a tentative green light—if so, this process may be simple. However, for most writers, this part of the publication process can be tedious and requires a great deal of patience—and the ability to handle rejection. It is all part of the game.

You do need to track where you send your queries or full proposals. If you get a call from a publisher and can't remember which house he is with—you will wish you had a quick check list close by. Send to as many publishers as appropriate. Simultaneous submissions are sometimes discouraged. I suggest that you ignore that advice, and don't rely on sending out one proposal package and waiting for a year to hear back before sending another. However, publishers do have a point—they don't want to spend a lot of time on your work just to learn you've gone with someone else. When you get an offer that is right for you, notify other publishers on your list.

Publisher Contacts

Publisher ⸻

Contact person/title ⸻

Address: ⸻

City ⸻ State ⸻ Zip ⸻

Telephone number ⸻ Fax ⸻

Email ⸻

Query letter (date sent/attach copy) ⸻

Proposal package (date sent/attach items you sent) ⸻

Publisher's response and date ⸻

Follow up to publisher's request (if any)

List of materials ⸻

Date sent ⸻

Publisher's response ⸻

Follow up ⸻

To-Do List

If you are working on a large project, it is easy to forget exactly who you met where—and what you promised you'd do. "Tell the mayor 'hello' for me," or "The museum director was my college roommate—ask her to tell you about the time we....." You get the idea.

Thank-you notes are always appreciated. Collect as many business cards as you can. They will provide correct spelling for the person's name, title, address and other information without taking the time to write it down while you are on site. It is worth your while to maintain contacts and build an ongoing professional relationship.

Not only are you writing a book, but you may want to write spinoff magazine articles, give speeches, or lead seminars on your subject. Your contacts can prove valuable for these efforts.

The following "to do" forms cover several topics. Adapt or create other forms as needed to fit your project:

- Thank-you notes – follow up. If you record the person's name/address/email while you are on site *and* the reason for a follow up, you'll find it easier to keep it all straight when you return to your office – or a week later when you have time to send your note.
- Return borrowed items. This chart will help keep the items you borrow and the information about the donor on track. I find jotting down the date I borrow and return an item provides a good reference if a problem arises.
- Miscellaneous list. You may need a "to call," "pick up," "facts to double check," "materials to send"—whatever your needs, a list helps.

To-Do List

Thank-You Notes

Person/title/address	Message subject	Date sent

Person/title/address	Message subject	Date sent

Person/title/address	Message subject	Date sent

Person/title/address	Message subject	Date sent

Person/title/address	Message subject	Date sent

Person/title/address	Message subject	Date sent

Return Borrowed Items

Person/title/address	Item	Date returned

Person/title/address	Item	Date returned

Person/title/address	Item	Date returned

Person/title/address	Item	Date returned

Person/title/address	Item	Date returned

Person/title/address	Item returned	Date returned

Person/title/address	Item returned	Date returned

Person/title/address	Item returned	Date returned

Miscellaneous Items

You may need a list of "to call" "pick up" "facts to double check" "materials to send"—whatever your needs, a list helps. List your item, date you took action, and follow up notes if needed. It is helpful to have a place to list these items as you go along rather than hunting for sticky notes or scribbled reminders to yourself on backs of envelopes.

Jobs to accomplish	Date complete	Follow up or N/A

Media Contacts

Develop your media contact list as you work on your book. Reporters are interested in upcoming projects and keeping them in the loop is useful. Check appropriate contacts for local and regional newspapers, local/regional/statewide magazines, newsletters of related organizations, lists of groups interested in your subject—as well as radio and television talk-show programs. Develop a list of emails, websites, and blogs you can contact when the book is finished. Keep your own blog and website up to date.

Talk to the Community Relations staff person at the large chain bookstores—and the owner of independent book stores. If you work with a publisher, much of this information may be sent to their publicity department; however, it is still going to be up to you to arrange many of your speaking engagements, seminar programs, book signings, and other means of promoting your book. You will probably need several pages for your contacts.

Media Contacts

Media	Contact Person	Information Sent	Date Sent	Response

INDEX

About the Author

M. H. Collins is an award-winning historian and freelance writer. Her passion for preserving local and regional history is fueled by an urgency to record people's stories before they are either forgotten or lost in upheavals in the community—good or bad.

As director of the Beaufort Historical Association in North Carolina, she co-authored *The Old Burying Ground: Beaufort, North Carolina*. This book won the Willie Parker Peace History Book Award from the North Carolina Society of Historians. Her next two books focus in Arkansas—*Rogers: The Town the Frisco Built*, a narrative nonfiction, and *Rogers, Arkansas*, a pictorial history. The latter book won first place for a nonfiction book by the Arkansas Press Women.

She is a former editor and current freelance writer for regional and national magazines. Her articles focus on travel, history, gardens, art, and writing skills. As owner of WilsonCollins Marketing and Management Consultants in the Washington DC area and North Carolina, she brought strong marketing skills to manage successful programs for corporations and non-profit groups. She brings these skills to her own writing ventures. Collins currently owns CHS Publishing.

Collins offers a stimulating workshop experience based on this book and other publishing experiences for those interested in improving their writing and organizational skills. Her presentations offer user-friendly marketing plans to help writers promote themselves and their work.

hswc1@cox.net—www.mhcollins.com

Order Form

Order by:

Email: hswc1@cox.net

Telephone: 1-479-903-6812.

Mail: CHS Publishing, P. O. Box. 1958, Rogers, AR 72757

Please send the book *Write History Right* **to:**

Name: _____

Address: _____

City: _____ State: _____ Zip: _____

Telephone: _____

Email address: _____

Number of copies _____ @ $16.95 per book $ _____

In Arkansas, 9% sales tax @ $1.53 per book $_____

            SUBTOTAL $_____

      Shipping: $4.00 per book $ _____

($2.00 shipping per book for multiple copies)

             TOTAL $_____

I have enclosed $ _____ Check number_____

Credit Card: ☐ MasterCard   ☐ Visa   ☐ Discover

          ☐ American Express

Name on credit card _____

Credit Card number _____

Four-digit confirmation number (back of card) _____

Expiration date _____

Print name shown on card _____

Signature _____